Elizabeth Van Lew

Southern Belle, Union Spy

Elizabeth Van Lew

Southern Belle, Union Spy

by Karen Zeinert

A People in Focus Book

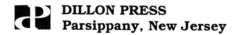
DILLON PRESS
Parsippany, New Jersey

To the Rosenbergs—Bob, Carol, Peter, Lisa, and Ann, and
Lyn and Tim McCarthy

Photo Credits

COVER: College of William & Mary. 12: Virginia State Library and
Archives. 21–25: The Valentine Museum, Richmond, Virginia. 27: College of
William & Mary. 31: © Schomberg Center for Research in Black Culture.
40: The Valentine Museum, Richmond, Virginia. 44: Massachusetts
Commandery Military Order of the Loyal Legion and the US Army Military
History Institute. 52: The Valentine Museum, Richmond, Virginia.
54: Massachusetts Commandery Military Order of the Loyal Legion and the
US Army Military History Institute. 58: The Valentine Museum, Richmond,
Virginia. 60: Van Lew Papers, New York Public Library. Manuscripts and
Archives Section. 67: The Virginia Historical Society. 69: Van Lew Papers,
New York Public Library. Manuscripts and Archives Section. 91: The Virginia
Historical Society. 93: The Valentine Museum, Richmond, Virginia.
105: Massachusetts Commandery Military Order of the Loyal Legion and the
US Army Military History Institute. 114: Van Lew Papers, New York Public
Library. Manuscripts and Archives Section. 121: Library of Congress.
122: Massachusetts Commandery Military Order of the Loyal Legion and the
US Army Military History Institute. 133: Van Lew Papers, New York Public
Library. Manuscripts and Archives Section. 138–140: The Virginia Historical
Society. 143: The Valentine Museum, Richmond, Virginia. 145: College of
William & Mary.

Library of Congress Cataloging-in -Publication Data

Zeinert, Karen.
    Elizabeth Van Lew: southern belle, Union spy / by Karen Zeinert.
  — 1st ed.
      p. cm. — (A people in focus book)
    Includes bibliographical references and index.

    ISBN 0-87518-608-4   ISBN 0-328-24960-7 pbk
      1. Van Lew, Elizabeth L., 1818–1900—Juvenile literature. 2. United
States—History—Civil War, 1861–1865—Secret service—
Juvenile literature. 3. Spies—United States—Biography—Juvenile litera-
ture. [1. Van Lew, Elizabeth L., 1818–1900. 2. Spies. 3. United States—
History—Civil War, 1861–1865—Secret service.]
I. Title II. Series.
E608.V34Z45   1995
973.7'85'092—dc20
[B]   94-27761

A biography of Elizabeth Van Lew, the Richmond, Virginia, woman who spied
for the North during the Civil War, and who supported rights for blacks and
for women.

Published by Dillon Press, an imprint of Silver Burdett Press.
A Simon & Schuster Company
299 Jefferson Road, Parsippany, NJ 07054

First edition

Printed in Mexico

/Contents

A Nation Divided

MAINE

MN

WISCONSIN

MICHIGAN

VT
NH
MA
NEW YORK
CT
RI

IOWA

PA
Gettysburg

NJ

UNION STATES

ILLNOIS   IN   OHIO

DELAWARE

Bull Run   Washington, D.C.

MARYLAND

MISSOURI

WV   VA   Cold Harbor

Appomattox   Richmond

KENTUCKY

Durham
Station

TENNESSEE   Raleigh   NC

Chattanooga

Atlantic
Ocean

ARKANSAS   Shiloh

Columbia

Atlanta   SC

CONFEDERATE STATES   Fort Sumter

MS   ALABAMA   GEORGIA

Vicksburg   Savannah

TEXAS   LOUISIANA

New Orleans

FL

Gulf of
Mexico

Legend:

- ☐ Union States
- ☐ Confederate States
- ☐ Territory
- 🔫 Battles
- ◄--- Sherman's march
- ○ Cities
- ✪ Union capital
- ✷ Confederate capital

Chapter / One

Some Background

When civil war broke out between America's Northern and Southern states in 1861, men in both parts of the nation were so eager to fight that they rushed to enlist. Both sides believed that the war would be short. More than anything, they feared it would end before they had a chance to see some action on the battlefield. But Northerners underestimated the South's courage and determination to fight against overwhelming odds, and Southerners misjudged the North's will to keep the Union (the United States) together. The short, glorious war everyone dreamed about turned into a nightmare, a four-year ordeal of hard-fought, bloody battles. By 1865, more than 600,000 men had died.

The North and South had been bitterly divided over several issues for many years. This division was a result of the fact that the two geographic sections, the industrialized North and the agricultural South, had very different needs. Although members of Congress from the two sections argued about issues such as taxation—how and where the money was to be spent—and how much power the federal government should have, it was the issue of slavery that drew the most attention and caused the most emotional debates.

Northerners wanted Congress to forbid slavery in the new territories and states that were being added to the country as it expanded west in the first half of the 1800s. Some wanted to outlaw slavery in the South as well. They believed the practice was morally wrong.

Southerners considered the North's stand on slavery a serious threat to their livelihood. The South needed many workers to produce tobacco and cotton, their major crops, and Southerners relied heavily on slave labor to work their fields. Slavery had existed in the South for more than two hundred years. By 1861, Southerners owned 3.5 million slaves. Since some slaves were valued at more than $1,000 each, few owners planned to set them free.

The issue of slavery was also tied to a struggle for power in Congress. Southern members of Congress wanted more slave states, whose representatives, they hoped, would vote with them. Their votes would enable the national legislature to pass laws that would help the South and protect slavery as well. But Northern congressmen refused to be outnumbered and overpowered, and congressional debates about the spread of slavery eventually became so heated that they often became shouting matches. Even though it was extremely difficult to do so, Congress managed to work out compromises in 1820 and 1850. Both agreements kept a balance between free and slave states, and neither group was able to dominate the legislature.

When more territories were added to the United States in the 1850s, Congress once again had to decide whether slavery would be allowed in those new territories. Emotions ran higher and higher with each debate, and some turned into nasty brawls. Members on both sides, fearing for their lives, actually carried knives and guns to congressional sessions to protect themselves.

At the same time, the number of abolitionists, people who wanted to end slavery completely, grew rapidly in the North. Southern leaders, realizing that the spread of slavery to new territories was doomed, knew that they would have less and less power in Congress. They feared that a Congress dominated by Northerners would eventually outlaw slavery altogether. To avoid this, they called on Southern states to secede, or leave, the United States.

Northerners—and a few Southerners such as Elizabeth Van Lew of Richmond, Virginia—were appalled by the very idea of secession. They vowed to do everything in their power to keep the Union together, even if it meant going to war. And many looked forward to the coming battles.

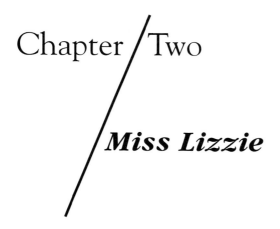

Chapter / Two

Miss Lizzie

When Elizabeth Van Lew picked up the newspaper in her Richmond, Virginia, mansion on February 27, 1865, she was confronted with shocking news. Confederate officers in Richmond had arrested two men in the Union spy ring she led. Both men had been charged with espionage. The men, William White and L. E. Babcock, had worked for the North for almost four years, and the news of their arrest was a devastating blow to Van Lew. The two loyal, experienced ring members would soon lose their lives. The Confederates hanged spies, and the very thought of Babcock and White dangling from nooses sick-

Elizabeth Van Lew

ened Van Lew, even though she had seen death many times in the past few years.

But the bad news didn't end with the headlines. As Van Lew read the article about Babcock and White, she realized that more trouble was in store. According to the paper, an informant had given Confederate officers a list of names of other members of the spy ring. At that very moment more Southern traitors were being rounded up.

High-strung by nature, her nerves frazzled by the constant pressure of trying to avoid arrest, Van Lew was overwhelmed by a moment of panic. Questions raced through her mind. How many had been identified? Would anyone try to save his or her own life by identifying other members? How many members would leave Richmond after reading the paper? In short, did she have an organization left?

But even though Elizabeth didn't have all the information she needed to answer her questions, there was one thing of which she was certain. She knew there was nothing she could do at the moment to help anyone. If her name had been mentioned—and she was reasonably sure it had been—she was probably being watched. Anyone she contacted now would come under suspicion, and she would only endanger the people she wanted to help. So she calmed herself and sat in her front parlor and waited to see if Confederate officers would come to arrest her. Meanwhile, she thought about Babcock and White and the only man who could have betrayed them, an Englishman named R. W. Pole.

Van Lew's latest crisis had started a few weeks earlier. By the beginning of February 1865, the North had cut off almost all outside supplies to the South, even food, and it had also beaten Southern forces in the western states of the Confederacy. The North was now concentrating on the South's army in the East, its last stronghold. Union leaders believed they would finally win the war if they could capture Richmond, the Confederate capital.

Information about the city at this time was especially important, and Union leaders never seemed to have enough contacts. So when a man calling himself Pole suddenly showed up in Union army headquarters in Washington, D.C., and volunteered to spy for the North in Richmond, Elizabeth's army contacts were happy to accept his services.

But getting to Richmond was not easy, since two lines of soldiers faced each other between the capitals. One line was made up of Northerners, and the other, closer to Richmond, was manned by Confederates. The inexperienced volunteer insisted that he couldn't possibly get through the South's line by himself or get started without aid. A messenger was sent south to ask Elizabeth to help Pole.

Van Lew was hesitant to do this. She had always insisted on working with people she knew well. She repeatedly questioned the messenger about Pole. How well did he know this volunteer? What made him believe that the Englishman was a Union supporter? Had anyone checked Pole's background?

White was also present when the messenger arrived. He, too, was hesitant to trust a stranger. White felt it was too risky to add a new person at the very time the spy ring was needed the most. He said that one mistake could ruin the ring and risk a dozen lives.

But the messenger was convinced that Pole was committed to their side, and he pleaded with Elizabeth. He said that Pole could help the Union because he was just the kind of man the Confederates would trust—smart and charming. And because he was English—and many Englishmen were sympathetic to the South's cause—Southerners would readily accept him. Finally, ignoring her instinct and better judgment,

Van Lew agreed to cooperate.

She ordered Babcock and White to bring Pole into Richmond. Shortly afterward, Babcock headed north to meet the Englishman and lead him through known holes in the South's line. It took several days to cover the distance, and the men hid in ring members' homes along the way. Babcock managed to get Pole into Richmond without any serious difficulty, and once they were in the city, the new spy was taken to a place of safety. The next morning, Babcock tended to some business after telling Pole to remain in hiding until White brought Confederate money and false identification papers for him.

However, Pole had no intention of waiting for White. In reality, the Englishman was a *Confederate* spy, and he had military secrets to pass on to Southern leaders in Richmond as soon as possible. He had tried to carry this information out of Washington for months, but he couldn't get through the Union lines, where the number of soldiers seemed to increase daily. Desperate—and clever—Pole then decided to take a step daring even for a spy. He would offer to work for the North in Richmond. If he were accepted, he knew that the Union would get him, and his information, past the North's guards, his real enemies.

Now Pole saw his chance to turn over his information, and he raced to Confederate headquarters in Richmond. Besides delivering his military secrets, Pole exposed the spy ring that had brought him into the capital. He told the Confederates about his guide, and he threw in every name he had heard Babcock mention as they traveled toward Richmond. He even gave the location of the homes in which he had stayed.

Although Pole's actions severely damaged Van Lew's organization, Elizabeth was miraculously spared for the moment. None of those arrested betrayed her even when Confederate officers threatened the spies' lives. When a gun was held to White's head and an officer threatened to blow his brains out if White wouldn't talk, White told him to go ahead and shoot. "Blood away!" he shouted. And if Pole had mentioned her name, the Confederate officers probably wouldn't have taken him seriously. Elizabeth had been accused of spying before, but no one had ever offered any proof. Real proof was needed to accuse someone like Van Lew. After all, Miss Lizzie, born and raised in the South, was a member of one of the city's most respected families.

Elizabeth's father, John Van Lew, was born in Jamaica, New York, in 1790. His ancestors came from Holland and Germany, arriving long before the Revolutionary War broke out, a war the Van Lew family actively supported. One of Mr. Van Lew's aunts carried messages from British-held New York to the patriots during that war until British guards caught and imprisoned her. Stories about John's aunt were passed on to Elizabeth, who was fascinated by her great-aunt's courage.

Mr. Van Lew received a fine education, and his parents hoped he would become a Latin professor. But he preferred business over teaching, and he went to work for a molasses merchant in New York as soon as he finished his schooling. He may have been on a business trip in Richmond in 1816 when he met Dr. John Adams. Van Lew, then twenty-six years old, and Dr. Adams decided to set up a commercial business of their own. It failed, and Van Lew's share of the debt was $100,000, no small sum in the 1800s!

Still full of ambition, John then became part-owner of the Van Lew & Taylor Hardware Store. This developed into an extremely successful business. After Van Lew paid off his debt, he and his partner enlarged their shop. Eventually, Elizabeth's father became the sole owner of the store, one of the largest in Virginia. By then he was a very wealthy man.

In 1817, Mr. Van Lew met Eliza Baker. They were married on January 10, 1818, in Dr. Adams's home, the same home they would buy a few years later.

Eliza Baker Van Lew, Elizabeth's mother, was a member of a prominent family in Pennsylvania. Eliza's ancestors, like her husband's, also had lived in the colonies during the Revolutionary War, and several had been involved in politics. Her father had helped draft Pennsylvania's first constitution, and he had served as mayor of Philadelphia. Like Mr. Van Lew, Eliza Baker had received a fine education, an unusual opportunity for a woman of that day.

Elizabeth, the oldest of the Van Lews' three children, was born on October 15, 1818, in Richmond. Miss Lizzie was a pretty, petite girl with blond hair and bright blue eyes. She was also strong willed. Her sister, Anna, was born two years later, and a brother, John, arrived in 1825.

What little is known about Elizabeth's early life indicates that she had a close, loving family and a happy childhood. She was especially fond of her father, who liked to read stories to his children from the family's large collection of books, a collection that grew annually. Mr. Van Lew set aside $50 each year to buy books, and his library included texts on politics and science as well as the best-known works of the day.

Like her parents, Elizabeth was well educated. She was tutored at home until she was seven years old, and then she was sent to Philadelphia to attend her mother's former school. She also had private lessons in music, dancing, horseback riding, and etiquette to enable her to join the best social circles in Richmond.

The Van Lews lived in a three-and-a-half story mansion situated on a large lot, a whole city block, on Church Hill. This mansion had been built from the finest materials available. It had many rooms, including two parlors to receive the family's numerous guests. Walls in most rooms were covered with brocaded silk, and huge crystal chandeliers provided light. Each room had a fireplace with an imported marble mantel and the best furniture available. Outside, wide graveled paths led to flower beds filled with masses of fragrant blooms and a rose garden. The Van Lews also owned a farm near the city. Their property, like that of most wealthy Southerners, was maintained by slaves.

Mr. and Mrs. Van Lew enjoyed giving dinner parties, and they must have been gracious hosts, for their invitations were eagerly sought and

The Van Lew mansion

quickly accepted. Besides serving a hearty meal on tables set with fine china and silver, the Van Lews often invited famous people of the day whom everyone wanted to meet: Actors, singers, and authors such as Edgar Allan Poe. Important politicians visited the Van Lews, too, and Elizabeth's father talked about current events with well-known men such as Jefferson Davis, the future president of the Confederacy.

Miss Lizzie was also very popular as a young woman, and she had an active social life. She held parties of her own in the mansion, and attended balls and garden parties at the homes of friends. She was driven to these gatherings in a fine carriage pulled by four snow-white horses.

Yet strangely enough, although Elizabeth was pretty and well liked, little is known about her romantic life. A family friend claimed that Elizabeth was in love with a young man who died, but she gave no details about him or his death. If this story is true, it might explain why Elizabeth never married. Brokenhearted, perhaps even a little bitter, she may have decided to discourage any more suitors.

On the other hand, young men may have considered Elizabeth a delightful dancing partner but a risky candidate for marriage. She was outspoken and independent at a time when women were expected to be quiet and dependent. For example, since women couldn't vote, they weren't supposed to be interested in politics. But not only was Elizabeth interested in how her country was being run; she had a few suggestions to make and she did so—out loud. In addition, Miss Lizzie did not look to others to make the rules by which she lived, and more than one would-be husband might have found her self-reliance rather daunting.

Major changes took place in the Van Lew mansion in the 1840s and 1850s. Mr. Van Lew died in 1843, and his sudden death was a great shock to Elizabeth. Her brother, John, took control of the store and successfully managed it for the family. Elizabeth, then twenty-five years old, assumed more duties in the mansion to help her mother during this difficult time. One year later, Elizabeth's sister married a doctor from Philadelphia and moved to that city. In 1854, John married, and he moved to a new home in Richmond.

A little lost without her brother and sister, Elizabeth decided she needed a change of scene. So in 1855, she went to Europe on a lengthy grand tour. She visited many countries, including Scotland, England, and France. Elizabeth, a dedicated gardener, collected flowers from the various places she visited, carefully drying and pressing them before mounting each blossom in her scrapbook. Such a trip was a rarity for Americans in those days, a privilege reserved only for those who could afford it—and who had an adventurous spirit.

When Elizabeth returned from Europe in the late 1850s, she made a momentous change at home. With her mother's blessing, she freed the family's slaves, most of whom chose to stay on as servants. Many in Richmond didn't realize, at first, anyway, what had happened. Elizabeth then began to buy the family members of her former slaves whenever they were offered for sale. She would free them and reunite the families. This action caught the attention of Richmonders and raised more than a few eyebrows in the city. Still, most people continued to think of Elizabeth as a solid citizen who just happened to have peculiar ideas about slavery.

Elizabeth's friends believed that she got her ideas about freeing slaves when she had gone to school in the North, and this is quite likely. While Elizabeth was in Philadelphia, antislavery people were very active in the city. These abolitionists wanted more supporters, and they published some dreadful stories about slavery, including tales of whippings and hangings for minor offenses. Elizabeth must have read some of these publications or heard about them in school, and they would have created a picture of slavery that was quite different from the one she had seen in her own home.

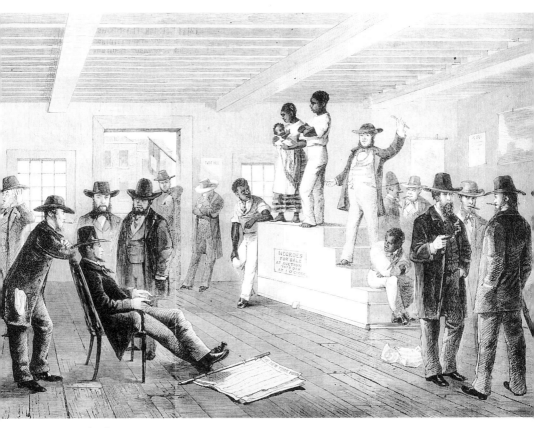

A slave auction

Elizabeth's feelings toward slavery also were affected by a tragic event at a slave auction. At first this auction, which took place while Elizabeth was in school in Philadelphia, was no different from others held regularly all over the South. Slaves for sale were led to a platform in the front of the auction room, where they were examined physically by would-be buyers—in full view of everyone present—before the sale began. When

the exams were finished, the slaves were presented, and buyers shouted out bids, the highest
bidder claiming the property. Everything went as
usual until a woman's baby was bought by a man
who refused to buy the mother as well. When the
baby was taken from the mother's arms, the
mother fell to her knees and died on the spot from
shock. The father of the baby was a former Van
Lew slave, and Elizabeth was heartsick when she
heard about this event.

As she learned more about slavery over the
years, Elizabeth came to hate it. She eventually
called slaveholders "cruel" and "arrogant," descrip-
tions that didn't sit well with her Southern
friends.

Elizabeth wasn't the only one whose attitude
toward slavery changed. Antislavery beliefs spread
rapidly in the 1850s, and the number of abolitionists in the North grew dramatically. Most of these
people did everything they could to end slavery
peacefully. They helped slaves escape to safety in
Canada and argued against laws that made it
easier for Southerners to capture runaways. They
also petitioned Congress to stop the spread of
slavery into newly opened territories.

While most abolitionists used peaceful means,
a handful turned to violence. In 1854, Congress—

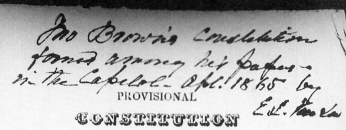

PROVISIONAL

CONSTITUTION

AND

ORDINANCES

FOR THE

PEOPLE OF THE UNITED STATES.

PREAMBLE.

Whereas, Slavery, throughout its entire existence in the United States, is none other than a most barbarous, unprovoked, and unjustifiable War of one portion of its citizens upon another portion ; the only conditions of which are perpetual imprisonment, and hopeless servitude or absolute extermination; in utter disregard and violation of those eternal and self-evident truths set forth in our Declaration of Independence : Therefore,

WE, CITIZENS OF THE UNITED STATES, AND THE OPPRESSED PEOPLE, WHO, BY A RECENT DECISION OF THE SUPREME COURT ARE DECLARED TO HAVE NO RIGHTS WHICH THE WHITE MAN IS BOUND TO RESPECT ; TOGETHER WITH ALL OTHER PEOPLE DEGRADED BY THE LAWS THEREOF, DO, FOR THE TIME BEING ORDAIN AND ESTABLISH FOR OURSELVES, THE FOLLOWING PROVISIONAL CONSTITUTION AND ORDINANCES, THE BETTER TO PROTECT OUR PERSONS, PROPERTY, LIVES, AND LIBERTIES ; AND TO GOVERN OUR ACTIONS:

ARTICLE I.

QUALIFICATIONS FOR MEMBERSHIP.

ALL persons of mature age, whether Proscribed, oppressed and enslaved Citizens, or of the Proscribed

John Brown was so certain of victory, he wrote a Constitution for a slave-free state that he hoped to start somewhere in the South.

tired of fighting over slavery—decided to let the people of the Kansas-Nebraska Territory vote on whether they wanted to be a free or a slave territory. Fighting broke out there between those who wanted slavery and those who didn't. In one incident, John Brown, a leader of a small antislavery group, led a bloody attack on proslavery men. He ordered his followers to use sabers to hack five men to death, and he watched as they did so. This attack was just the beginning of Brown's crusade. The real battle, if all went as the abolitionist hoped, was yet to come.

Chapter / Three

Which Side Are You On?

On a chilly, moonless night in October 1859, John Brown and eighteen of his followers were once again ready for action, this time just outside Harpers Ferry, Virginia. Brown planned to seize weapons stored in a federal armory there to free and arm as many slaves as he could for an all-out rebellion. After surveying the scene one last time, he ordered the attack. His followers cut telegraph lines, blocked exits from town, seized hostages, and took over federal property containing several million dollars' worth of guns and ammunition.

But events didn't go exactly as Brown had planned. A doctor in Harpers Ferry ran for help after he managed to get past Brown's men, and before the abolitionists could free a single slave, local and federal troops rushed in. Ten of the raiders were killed or fatally wounded. The rest, including Brown, were captured by U.S. Marines under the temporary command of Colonel Robert E. Lee. Shortly afterward, John Brown was tried, found guilty of treason, and hanged.

Southerners were stunned by Brown's raid. There was little they feared more than a slave rebellion, and although all revolts in the past had eventually failed, one in Virginia in 1831 had turned into a bloody massacre before it was put down. At least sixty people had died, including slaveholders' wives and children. Southerners had watched their slaves more closely after the 1831 rebellion, and slaveowners thought they had everything under control—until Brown began his crusade.

Southerners were also stunned by Northerners' reaction to the raid. Many called Brown a hero, and they rang bells and fired guns throughout the North at the hour of his execution to show their support for his actions. These activities were reported in Southern newspapers, and many editorials argued that all Northerners were sympathetic to Brown. Northerners intended to end slavery by

John Brown

force, editors cried out, and the next time they might be successful!

Readers believed these editors, and rumors about upcoming raids were common. At one point, it was said that the whole North would attack, and Southerners were overwhelmed by panic. Local citizens decided to protect themselves and their property by organizing home guard associations just in case the North did attack. Even though no raids occurred, Southerners still felt threatened.

They felt even more threatened when Abraham Lincoln was elected president in 1860. They believed that Lincoln was an abolitionist and that he would convince Congress to end slavery. Lincoln was so feared—and detested—in the South that he didn't receive a majority of votes in any slave state. Southerners saw his election as further proof that the North wanted to end slavery. Why else, they wondered, did Northerners vote for such a candidate? Southerners shook their heads in amazement at the results of the election, recalling the president-elect's love of jokes and rather colorful stories and his unkempt appearance. Why, he was nothing more than a buffoon, they said, a joker who was unfit to lead them.

Although some Southern leaders had talked

for years about seceding, most Southerners didn't consider the situation serious enough to justify leaving the Union. But by the late 1850s, many began to view secession as the only solution to the conflict between the industrial North and the agricultural South. If they seceded, they argued, they would be able to make their own decisions instead of having to abide by a federal government dominated by Northerners. More important, they would be able to preserve their way of life. They believed they had the legal right to secede since, in their opinion, the Constitution was simply an agreement between states to form a government. This agreement, they said, could be broken when the safety and happiness of a state's citizens were threatened.

Northern leaders interpreted the Constitution differently. They said that no state had the right to leave under any circumstances. According to Northerners, secession was a blow at the basic democratic idea that the majority should rule. If Southern states could leave when they didn't have their way, what, Northerners asked, would prevent others from doing the same?

But despite Northern arguments for unity, Southern states began to secede in late 1860. In February 1861, representatives from Alabama,

Florida, Georgia, Louisiana, Mississippi, South Carolina, and Texas met to form a new nation, the Confederate States of America. After electing Jefferson Davis president, they invited the rest of the slave states—Arkansas, Delaware, Kentucky, Maryland, North Carolina, Tennessee, and Virginia—to join them.

On February 13, Virginians sent delegates to a convention in Richmond to decide on the fate of their state. In the beginning, those who wished to remain in the Union outnumbered those who wanted to leave by two to one. Those in the majority who were staunch Unionists urged the secessionists to remain loyal to their country. Others in the majority who backed the right to secede felt that Virginia did not have sufficient cause to withdraw yet, and they, too, argued for remaining in the Union. But the minority was not convinced by either plea, and its speakers demanded that Virginia secede. The debates were very long and very emotional.

Like many citizens in Richmond, Elizabeth attended all debates open to the public. She was deeply moved by the speakers, many of whom were overwhelmed by the thought of leaving a country they loved. "I have listened to words of burning eloquence in the convention," she wrote in a journal she started after John Brown's raid, "and seen tears in the eyes of many of the members."

The arguing continued for two months, and during that time, secession supporters in the convention and on the streets became more and more aggressive. Many wanted to run all Union supporters out of town or, at the very least, burn their homes. Some thought these punishments were too lenient. They wanted to hang Northern sympathizers. Understandably, fewer and fewer pleas were given for not seceding.

Although Elizabeth stopped arguing against secession as threats against Union supporters increased, her loyalty to the Union never wavered. She could never support the Confederate cause as long as it wanted to preserve slavery. Also, she didn't believe that a state had the right to secede, and she thought that any person who wanted to destroy the Union was a traitor. Her antisecession position, like her antislavery stand, could have been the result of her Northern education or the result of listening to arguments at the convention. In either case, it was a deeply held belief.

Delegates were still debating in Richmond when Union and Confederate soldiers exchanged shots at Fort Sumter, South Carolina, on April 12,

1861. Confederates had surrounded all federal arsenals in the seceding states, and they had demanded that the properties be turned over to the Confederacy. Although most commanders did so immediately, Union forces at Fort Sumter refused to leave their post. When Northern reinforcements tried to join the men in the fort, Southerners fired on them. Most Americans considered this the beginning of war.

Most of Richmond's citizens—certain they would soon be part of the Confederacy—celebrated the outbreak of war by ringing church bells and setting off elaborate displays of fireworks. Meanwhile, Elizabeth wept at the thought of Americans killing one another.

Shortly afterward, President Lincoln issued a call for 75,000 men, and he asked Virginia to send troops. The fact that Lincoln planned to use force against the seceding states pushed every delegate from Virginia who believed that a state had the right to secede into the Confederate camp. On April 17, delegates decided to end the debate and cast their ballots. The vote was eighty-eight to fifty-five in favor of secession.

Most of the fifty-five votes against secession were cast by men from the western counties in Virginia. When these men returned home, they held another convention. They decided not to leave the Union, and the area they represented seceded from Virginia, eventually becoming the state of West Virginia.

Virginia's secession was a great morale booster for the South. The state's resources included the largest flour mills in the world, huge ironwork factories, and a strong militia. Also, its northern border was only a few miles from Washington, D.C., placing the North's capital within easy striking range.

When Virginia's delegates announced their decision to secede, citizens of Richmond prepared a grand celebration. Announcements of a parade appeared in the city's papers, and everyone was encouraged to join in.

When the appointed time arrived, thousands of jubilant Richmonders, carrying blazing torches, marched up and down the streets. A few men were given the privilege of leading the procession, and each man was allowed to bear the front torch for one block before passing it on to the next in line. Occasionally the men and women paused next to platforms to listen to speakers who predicted a quick victory for the Confederate troops. After roaring their approval, they moved on, shouting and singing as they went. Fireworks lit up the sky, and windows in homes and businesses glowed throughout the city, illuminated by countless candles. It was a breathtaking sight.

Elizabeth sadly watched the procession from her home. Unlike the paraders, she had little to celebrate, and their joy was in stark contrast to her pain. They rejoiced that they were no longer citizens of the United States. She wept over that knowledge. They linked arms with their friends, sharing the momentous occasion with one another beneath the bright torchlights. She stood in the darkness alone.

Emotionally overwhelmed at one point, she sought refuge in her garden, seeking the strength she needed to face a difficult future. Although she had the means to seek safety in the North, Elizabeth was not the kind of person who would run away from a problem, no matter how serious it might be. In addition, she couldn't abandon her beloved family home. She wouldn't abandon her principles, either, yet she knew that if she remained in Richmond, she would be persecuted for her beliefs. Did she have the courage, she wondered aloud, to stand up to everyone she knew, neighbors, good friends, and bullies? After several hours of deliberation, many prayers, and countless tears, she found the strength she sought. "Never," she wrote later in her journal, "did a feeling of more calm determination . . . come over me."

Although Elizabeth had made her support for the Union quite clear, her friends still hoped that she would change her mind after Virginia seceded, for the pressures to do so were great. At the beginning of the war, loyalty to one's state was very strong, and people supported whatever side their delegates voted to join. This was even true of men in the U.S. Army. Many Southern soldiers and officers resigned when their states left the Union, and they joined Confederate militias. Robert E. Lee, for example, left his command in the U.S. Army, turning down an offer to lead the North's troops, when Virginia seceded. Instead, he became the commander of the Army of Northern Virginia.

Shortly after Virginia joined the Confederacy, several women visited Elizabeth and her mother. As usual, the Van Lews served their guests tea and a variety of fancy cakes, and they talked about events happening in Richmond. Then one of the visitors asked the Van Lews if they would help the men from Virginia. The visitors, one lady explained, were forming a sewing circle to make shirts for the men, and the women were looking for volunteers to help them.

Elizabeth didn't hesitate in her reply. In a

firm voice, she announced that she and her mother—who had agreed to support her daughter's decision not to help the South—were Union supporters. They would not make shirts for Confederate soldiers.

The visitors stared in astonishment at Elizabeth. They had given her one last chance to join them, and she had actually refused. This was more than the women could tolerate. Elizabeth had been outspoken in her beliefs about slavery, and they had overlooked it. She had argued that Virginia should remain in the Union, and they had overlooked that, too. But now Miss Lizzie actually had turned her back on their beloved Virginia, and worst of all, she had persuaded her mother to do the same. The women rose and left the mansion without saying a word.

As Elizabeth and her mother watched their visitors leave, they realized that the moment Elizabeth had dreaded had arrived. It wouldn't be long before Richmonders all over the city closed their doors on the Van Lews. The once socially prominent mother and daughter, who loved company, were now very much alone.

Robert E. Lee

Chapter / Four

No Place for a Lady

As the jubilant citizens of Richmond prepared for war, Elizabeth watched them with amazement. She wondered if they really understood the terrible price they, especially, would pay for seceding from the Union. Virginia would be a principal battleground. Not only was it one of the northernmost states in the Confederacy, standing guard over a good part of the South, but seizing the city of Richmond itself would be an important goal for the Union. Richmond had been designated the capital of the Confederacy, replacing the temporary capital located in Montgomery, Alabama. In fact, "On to Richmond!" slogans had already been shouted out in Northern rallies by those who believed that the fall of the capital would mean the fall of the Confederacy.

Part of the preparations Elizabeth witnessed included raising an army for Virginia. A massive recruiting campaign was started, and it seemed as if new regiments were organized daily. More than forty thousand volunteers from all over the state joined up, and they crowded into Richmond for training and supplies, outnumbering the citizens of the capital by more than ten thousand people.

Meanwhile, Virginia's leaders tried to figure out how to obtain the armaments needed for battle. One of the biggest manufacturing plants in the South was Richmond's Tredegar Iron Works, and rush orders were immediately placed at its office for guns and cannon. The factory quickly began to produce both in large quantities, manufacturing more than ten thousand cannon during the war. Tredegar made arms for troops not only from Virginia but for all of the Confederacy, giving Northerners one more reason for wanting to capture the city.

Military leaders in Richmond struggled to keep order among the throngs of men arriving daily. Volunteers were assigned to units, trained as quickly as possible, and taken out of the city to defend the Confederacy's northern border.

In addition to Virginia's soldiers, units from all over the South poured into the city for the antici-

Tredegar Iron Works in Richmond, Virginia, became the chief cannon maker for the Confederacy.

pated battle for the capital. Although their presence was welcome, they added to the confusion. And despite careful planning, the city's streets were usually clogged with carts carrying supplies for the units or jammed with long lines of soldiers going north. Often well-wishers lined the streets as soldiers left the city. Men, women, and children cheered and sang patriotic songs as the troops passed by.

One of the most popular songs was the "Marseillaise," a rousing march from the French Revolution. New words were written to the old tune and printed in local papers so everyone could learn them. The song, especially the militant chorus, resounded through the streets of Richmond:

> *To arms! to arms! ye brave!*
> *The avenging sword unsheath!*
> *March on! march on! all hearts resolved,*
> *For victory or death!*

Local newspapers also ran emotional editorials, encouraging Southerners to fight. The *Virginia Sentinel* of May 20, 1861, was typical when it said: Courage fellow citizens! Away with the croaker [doubter]—let him turn and flee! . . . We can't be conquered. We must triumph! Let all . . . resolve to

> 'Strike—til the last armed foe expires!
> *Strike—for our altars and our fires,*
> *Strike—for the green graves of our Sires,*
> *God and our native land!'*

Although Elizabeth said little on the streets of Richmond about her beliefs and feelings, which would have made her a "croaker" at best, she said plenty in her journal. And she was particularly harsh toward Richmond's women. She thought that ladies were unrealistic about how easy it would be to leave the Union. On one occasion she wrote, "The women became its [the secession's] strongest advocates, unknowing and unreflecting."

Elizabeth also thought that the women were bloodthirsty. Their plea, "Kill as many Yankees [Northerners] as you can for me," disgusted her. Although it is doubtful that the women really expected to receive a bloody trophy of war, Elizabeth noted that they asked for President Lincoln's head and if that wasn't possible, then a piece of his ear would do.

Even though several skirmishes took place shortly after the South seceded, the Battle at Bull Run, in July 1861, was the first official confrontation of the war. Major General McDowell, under orders from President Lincoln, moved southward with more than 30,000 men to force 23,000 Confederates from an important railhead less than twenty miles southwest of Washington, D.C. The two armies met in force on July 17. Confederate soldiers not only held their ground but forced McDowell's men to retreat. Northerners raced pell-mell back to Washington, where government officials wrung their hands in anxiety, believing that Confederate soldiers would appear in the capital at any moment.

Southerners, of course, rejoiced when they received word of their victory at Bull Run. More than one person now believed that the backbone of the war was broken and that peace was near. As a result, many Southerners underestimated the North's ability to fight, a serious mistake.

Although the citizens of Richmond were as jubilant as anyone else in the South when victory was announced, once Confederate soldiers began to arrive in the city, rejoicing turned to painful reality. More than 1,600 wounded were brought to the capital. Bleeding and mangled, missing arms and legs—even parts of their faces, they were carried into the city ahead of the bodies of the 400 Southern soldiers who had died in the battle.

Local hospitals couldn't possibly take care of all the wounded, and officials had to turn to volunteers for help. Citizens were asked to take in soldiers, and medical students were assigned to private homes to help care for the wounded. Officials also asked the women of the city to cook food and bring it to the hospitals. Meanwhile, requests for medical supplies were relayed to sewing circles, where officials hoped ladies would roll bandages as well as make shirts.

But wounded Confederate soldiers were less than half of the people who suddenly needed care and supervision. The South had taken more than one thousand prisoners, a number of whom were wounded. When the prisoners arrived in the capital, guards had great difficulty restraining the local people. So many wanted to see "real live Yankees" that it was difficult to make room through the crowd so that the prisoners could march—or in the case of the wounded, be carried—to prisons or tobacco warehouses. These facilities would serve as temporary prisons.

Not all of those captured were soldiers, however. Anticipating a decisive battle, citizens on both sides had piled into carriages and ridden out to view the fight at Bull Run. This group included a senator from Massachusetts who brought along a pair of dancing shoes for a victory ball he planned to host in Richmond after the battle.

Two members of Congress from the North, Alfred Ely and Calvin Huson Jr., were also present at the battle. Unlike the senator from Massachusetts—who left his dancing shoes on the battlefield when he ran for safety—the representatives were captured at Bull Run and taken to Richmond, where they were confined to Libby Prison. When Richmonders learned that congressmen were being held, they flocked to the prison to get a glimpse of the men. Some even offered to pay guards $10 to let them enter the building to see the politicians.

Northern prisoners were treated relatively

well in the beginning of the war, when supplies were abundant and people believed the war would be short and glorious. To show their compassion for all humanity, Southern women took food and clothing to the wounded prisoners, and they nursed those who were sick. For most, it was simply an extension of what Southerners had long been known for: their gracious hospitality.

But when Congressman Huson became ill with typhoid fever, Elizabeth Van Lew went one step further than most Richmonders who helped Northern prisoners. She asked for—and received—permission to take him to her mansion, where she and her mother could care for him. Even though Huson received the best treatment possible under the circumstances, he died shortly after being moved.

Elizabeth then arranged to hold his funeral in her home. Huson's friend Congressman Ely was allowed to leave prison for a few hours to attend the service. Although Miss Lizzie's help for Huson got lots of attention and caused some tongues to wag, no one harassed her.

Prisoners in Richmond organized the Richmond Prison Association, and shortly after Huson's death, the men sent a letter expressing heartfelt thanks to Elizabeth and her mother for the help the women had given to the congressman. Elizabeth treasured this letter, and it was found among her papers after her death.

As word about the Van Lews' kind treatment of Huson spread throughout the association, Union prisoners learned to trust the two women. This would be of benefit in the coming months to Elizabeth, the men, and the Union.

Bull Run was not the decisive battle that some Southerners had predicted it would be. In the coming months, as more dead and wounded Confederates were carried into Richmond and more Northern soldiers were captured, the attitude toward Union prisoners changed dramatically. Stories about overcrowding and poor treatment in the prisons began to circulate about the city, and fewer and fewer women were willing to help the prisoners.

Also, tales about poor prison food—or little food—became commonplace as supplies in Richmond dwindled. This shortage was partly the result of the naval blockade that the Union set up to prevent any food or arms from being brought into the South. The blockade was started in mid-April 1861, and it was very effective. The South could not fight the line of ships patrolling the Confederacy's coast because it didn't have a navy.

Rumors about starvation became so common that Northern officials insisted on sending representatives to Richmond to check on the prisoners' well-being, a demand that Richmond officials considered an insult.

To increase food supplies for a war that was now certainly going to last longer than sixty days, Southern farmers switched their crops from tobacco and cotton to something people could eat. But it took months to raise new produce, and in the meantime, everyone in the South either had to pay more for scarce items or do without.

Elizabeth had heard the stories about the living conditions in the city's four prisons: Libby, Belle Isle, Castle Thunder, and Castle Goodwin. Fully aware that the attitude toward anyone helping the prisoners had turned for the worst, she still was determined to help the men, and in doing so, to help the Union as well. But first she needed a pass to enter the prisons.

She called on Lieutenant David H. Todd. He was a half brother of Mary Todd Lincoln, President Lincoln's wife. (Mrs. Lincoln's father had married twice. Children born during the first marriage remained loyal to the Union. Children from the second marriage joined the Confederate cause.) Lieutenant Todd was shocked by

Elizabeth's request for permission to care for
Union prisoners. He told her that he knew men
who would gladly shoot them! He could not—
would not!—allow a lady such as Miss Lizzie to
have any contact with Yankees.

But Elizabeth wasn't about to give up. She
then visited Secretary of the Treasury C. G.

Belle Isle Prisoners, an engraving by Thomas Nast

Memminger, a man whom she had met before, to see if he could assist her. Memminger was just as shocked as Lieutenant Todd had been by her request. He told her that prison was no place for a lady. Elizabeth just smiled. She told Memminger that she had heard him speak eloquently about religion and Christian love. In one of his speeches he had stated that Christians were supposed to show their love for humanity through acts of kindness to the thankless and unworthy. Wasn't this, she wondered, a perfect opportunity to do so? Memminger could hardly disagree with such a plea when his own arguments were being used. He gave Elizabeth a note to take to Provost Marshal John H. Winder, the general in charge of prisons and police in Richmond.

Elizabeth then went to Winder, a man whom many considered vain and arrogant. Here she also used praise to get what she wanted. Noticing how the light in the room flattered Winder's beautiful white hair, she told him, "Your hair would adorn the Temple of Janus [a Roman god]. It looks out of place here."

Winder gave her the pass. It entitled her to offer prisoners books, food, and even delicacies. This pass was the first of many she would receive from the general.

A Richmond street where Van Lew would have walked to the prisons

Elizabeth and her mother soon became daily shoppers in the market, and their wealth made it possible for them to buy fresh fruits and vegetables, no matter what the cost might be. They also hauled basket upon basket of fresh produce in from their farm outside the city. Few in Richmond believed that petite Elizabeth and her frail mother were eating all that food, and it wasn't long before everyone realized that the Van Lews were feeding Yankees. In addition, Richmonders learned that the women were giving the prisoners paper and pens so they could write to their families, lending them books from their extensive library, and bringing in doctors—at the Van Lews' expense— to care for the sick.

The community reacted to the Van Lews' actions with great anger. Elizabeth wrote, "The threats, the scowls, the frowns of an infuriated community, who can write them? I have had brave men shake their fingers in my face and say terrible things!" One of the men not only waved a finger in her face; he hinted that some punishment was being planned for her.

Shortly afterward, Elizabeth received two notes. The first, decorated with a skull and crossbones, was addressed to "Old Maid" and signed by the "White Caps," a secret organization that harassed Unionists in Richmond. This note asked Van Lew if her house was insured. The second note warned her that the White Caps were coming soon, and the writer drew a picture of Elizabeth's house in flames. Although the organization threatened Van Lew several times, its threats were not carried out.

Articles in local newspapers also threatened the Van Lews:

Two ladies, mother and daughter, living on Church Hill, have lately attracted public notice by their . . . attentions to the Yankee prisoners. Whilst every true woman in this community has been busy making articles for

*our troops, or administering to our sick, these
two women have been spending their opulent
means in aiding and giving comfort to the mis-
creants [villains] who have invaded our sacred
soil, bent on . . . murder. . .. Out upon all
pretexts to humanity! The course of these two
females, in providing . . . delicacies, bringing
. . . books, stationery and paper, cannot but
be regarded as an evidence of sympathy
amounting to an endorsement of the cause and
conduct of these Northern vandals.*

Another article suggested that Elizabeth and
her mother get out of town while the getting was
good. "This is a warning to certain females . . . of
decidedly Northern proclivities [sympathies]. If
such people do not wish to be exposed and dealt
with as . . . enemies to their country they would do
well to cut stick [leave] with their worthless
carcass[es] while they can do so with safety."

New rumors about the Van Lews appeared
almost daily, and they had a devastating effect on
Mrs. Van Lew, who was now in her early sixties.
When Mrs. Van Lew heard that she and her
daughter were about to be arrested because they
supposedly were dealing in Union dollars, her
health began to fail. Elizabeth then decided she

should at least try to make life a little more comfortable for her mother. In a rare turnabout, Miss Lizzie volunteered to take hymnals to Confederate soldiers in Richmond. She noted later that it added to the soldiers' comfort as well as to the Van Lews'—for a while.

Ironically, Richmonders were angry at Elizabeth for all the food and supplies she was carrying into the Yankee prison. They should have been a lot more concerned about what she was carrying out.

John Henry Winder

B rigadier General John Henry Winder had a
long career in the U.S. Army. He graduated
from the West Point
Military Academy in
1820.   Winder
taught at the
academy for
three years
and fought
in the war
b e t w e e n
M e x i c o
and   the
U n i t e d
States from
1846-1848.
He resigned
from the U.S.
Army to support
the Confederacy in
1861.

Shortly afterward, Winder became provost
marshal of Richmond. He was responsible for all
Union prisoners brought into the city, all
Southern deserters caught and brought back to the

capital, and every thief, drunk, and prostitute in the area, whose numbers, according to newspapers of the time, grew rapidly. One article claimed that every scoundrel in the Confederacy had found his way to Richmond—where, in the beginning of the war, jobs and money were plentiful.

Winder had a difficult task and lots of critics. He hired many men with little training from Baltimore, his home city, rather than local men whom the citizens trusted. This caused deep resentment in Richmond. Critics called Winder's men Pug-uglies. Pug was a slang term for a fist fighter. Apparently Winder's men had numerous scraps with local citizens who refused to obey the "ugly" outsiders. Also, Richmonders regarded Winder's men as ineffective at best. As the crime rate soared, they sneered at Winder and argued that his men spent too much time harassing locals for passes—no one could leave town without one—and not enough time catching criminals. Prisoners of war thought he was cruel. They blamed Winder for their food shortages and over-crowding, and they actually cheered when news of the provost marshal's death reached the prisons in February 1865.

Gifts from Prisoners

Union prisoners in Richmond showed their appreciation for all that Elizabeth did for them by presenting her with gifts. Since the men lacked both money and any opportunity to buy something, most of their gifts were limited to what they could make from the few resources available to them. Some of the men, for instance, wrote poems. Others made pieces of jewelry, a ring or a pair of studs (decorative pins for clothing with posts and backings similar to those found on earrings for pierced ears), from frag-ments of meat bones. One pair of studs was decorated with Union flags.

If men lacked the materials or skills to make a gift, they gave Van Lew personal items to show her how much her care meant to them. One of the most touching gifts Elizabeth received was a photo of a soldier's daughter. It was all the soldier had to offer, and it must have been a great sacrifice to part with it.

Van Lew treasured these gifts the rest of her life, and after she died, they were eventually added to historical collections. The poems, part of Van Lew's scrapbook, were copied, and these copies can be found in the Earl Gregg Swem Library at the College of William and Mary in Williamsburg, Virginia. A copy of the letter accompanying the little girl's picture is also part of this collection. Several pieces of jewelry are now part of the Van Lew Collection in the New York Public Library.

Chapter / Five

The Spying Business

While Elizabeth distributed food and books to Yankee prisoners, she picked up pieces of information here and there that she knew would be of value to Union generals. It isn't clear whether she actually sought information at first. But once she had the material, she willingly sent it on, even though doing so endangered her life.

At some point though, Elizabeth eagerly and actively began to gather information. What she said in her messages to the Union generals isn't any more certain than when she said it, for after the war ended, she asked to have all her messages returned to her. Since none of these has ever been found, it's assumed that she destroyed them. Also, she eventually tore out pages, even whole sections, from her journal and burned them to destroy evidence of espionage. She did this to protect both herself and those with whom she worked. But no matter when she started to gather information, it is clear from her remaining notes and letters and other historical sources that she used a variety of means to get the facts she needed.

At first, Elizabeth was allowed to talk to the prisoners quite freely. Many of these men had seen a lot on their way to Richmond, and they had also picked up pieces of information from their guards or a doctor or a Southern deserter. By themselves, these pieces often meant little, but when they were put together, they were quite valuable. And as long as Van Lew could visit the prisons, she had an unending source of information.

But in mid-January 1862, Elizabeth received a letter telling her that she could no longer enter the prisons. The doctor in charge of Richmond's prisoners had decided that volunteers should no longer take food to the Yankees, and soldiers had been instructed to refuse to accept her old pass. This decision was backed by the Confederacy's war department and Provost Marshal Winder.

Appalled once again by the Confederates' lack of humanity and frustrated over her loss of information, Elizabeth immediately began to make plans to get a new pass. She marched to the office of the Confederacy's assistant secretary of war, A. E. Bledsoe, with a big bowl of her rich custard under her arm, hoping to win him over with the treat.

After downing the custard, Bledsoe agreed that it would do the prisoners some good to have such nourishing food. He saw no reason to deny her a pass, and he agreed to help her get permission to enter the prisons again. On January 24, he sent Van Lew a note indicating that he would try to talk to Provost Marshal Winder on her behalf. Bledsoe was successful, and Elizabeth was able to see the prisoners again.

Bledsoe may not have seen any danger in letting Elizabeth into the prisons, but the guards saw her as a real threat. For one thing, they thought she talked to the Yankees too much. What, they wondered, could she possibly have to say to prisoners? More important, what were the prisoners saying to her? To prevent the Yankees from giving out information, the guards told Van Lew that she could no longer speak to the Northerners, and guards stood nearby while she visited each prisoner to make sure that no conversation took place.

Although this made Elizabeth's task more difficult, it didn't stop her from getting the information she wanted. She simply devised several silent ways to ask questions and receive answers.

One method involved using a double-bottomed metal dish. In the past when she brought hot food into the prison, she had kept the food warm in a dish that had two compartments. The lower compartment held hot water, and the upper portion contained the food. Now, from time to time, Elizabeth omitted the water and slipped a message into the bottom portion instead. When the prisoners reached out for the dish and felt cool metal, they knew there was a message inside. As soon as possible, they removed the paper, wrote their answers, and returned the paper to its hiding place.

This dish passed back and forth between Elizabeth and the prisoners so often that one of the guards decided he should take a look at it. While talking to another guard, he muttered something about checking that container the next time Van Lew entered the prison, and Elizabeth overheard the comment.

She returned with the dish a few days later. This time she had filled the bottom to the brim with boiling water and had wrapped it in a shawl. When the guard asked to see the container, Van Lew politely declined, saying it was especially hot today. The soldier wasn't about to be put off, however, and he demanded to see the dish. Van Lew then pulled back the shawl and held out the dish for inspection. After grabbing the container and juggling it like a hot potato to avoid burning his hands, the guard spilled most of the water on himself. His howls could be heard in a large portion of the prison. He never asked to see the dish again.

Elizabeth also used books to pass and receive information. Although guards checked her texts for any signs of writing or loose slips of paper, they didn't look for pin marks. Both Van Lew and the men marked key words and numbers with tiny pin holes. When the pages were held in front of a candle, the holes could easily be seen.

Although gathering intelligence in the prisons may not have been Van Lew's primary reason for entering them—she spent a large part of her fortune on food, medicine, and other supplies for prisoners—her second source for information was deliberately infiltrated. This source was the Confederate White House.

When the South decided to make Richmond its capital in 1861, Confederate officials began to move to the city, including the Confederacy's president, Jefferson Davis. Davis needed more servants for his new home, and he began to ask

Jefferson Davis

Richmonders for recommendations. When Van Lew heard that the president was looking for help, she contacted Davis, who had known her father, and she offered to provide him with a good servant, an offer he accepted.

Elizabeth then sent for Mary Elizabeth Bowser, a former Van Lew slave. Elizabeth had noted Bowser's intelligence early on, and after freeing the girl, she sent her to Philadelphia to be educated at the Van Lews' expense. Now Elizabeth asked her to come back to Richmond to take on a dangerous job. Van Lew wanted her to work as a servant in the Davis household and spy on the president. Bowser agreed to do this, and after a short training period with Elizabeth, the former slave began to work for the Davises.

But getting information out of prison or Jefferson Davis's house was only part of the task. Elizabeth had to get her material into the Union's hands. Although her first information, incredibly enough, was simply sent through the mail, Van Lew could hardly continue to do this. She then began to develop a better system for sending intelligence to Washington.

First of all, she took steps to protect the information. She wrote her messages in code. That way, if a messenger was caught with a note, the information it contained might be safe. (The messenger, however, could expect lots of trouble. Carrying coded letters during the war was considered most suspicious and reason enough for arrest.) Elizabeth hid her code behind a picture of her mother in a lavaliere watch, a locket-like timepiece she wore about her neck at all times.

Toward the end of the war, Elizabeth went one step further to protect the information. She wrote all correspondence in code in invisible ink furnished by the Union. Messages written in this ink became visible when treated with milk.

After the message was written in code, it was taken out of Richmond to the Van Lew farm as soon as possible by one of several couriers. Sometimes Elizabeth carried the message herself. She had obtained a pass from Winder, which was necessary to get past guards posted outside the city, so she supposedly could check on things on the farm. This enabled her to go back and forth between her mansion and farm often.

On other occasions, one of the servants, a former Van Lew slave, carried the information in a hollowed-out heel of a shoe when he or she was

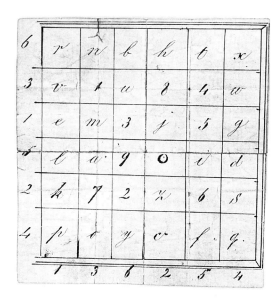

The code used by Elizabeth Van Lew in writing messages to Union commanders

sent to the farm to get fresh eggs and vegetables. Since fresh produce was needed often—especially as the war progressed and food became more and more scarce—frequent trips by servants to the farm did not arouse suspicion.

Occasionally, a seamstress who lived outside Richmond hid the information among her patterns cut from tissue paper. After fitting Elizabeth for a new dress, the seamstress carried the messages out of the city as she returned home. The coded information was punched into the patterns with pins. Since patterns were pinned to fabric when a dress was cut out and often were used more than one time, the messages blended in with the many holes already present, and they didn't raise any curiosity among the guards on the city's outskirts.

The Van Lew farm was only the first of several relay stations where messages were passed on to another courier. There were two more stations between Richmond and Union headquarters. The location of these varied, depending upon Confederate surveillance. By the end of the war, Elizabeth's system was able to function so smoothly that flowers picked from her garden one afternoon and sent along with the message appeared in Union headquarters the next morning.

Besides former slaves, Elizabeth had a number of Richmonders in her ring. She had known some of these people before the war, and she met others at the secession debates. Her Northern contacts also directed her to other spies in the city who were working on their own. In addition to Babcock and White, who were exposed by Pole, she worked with two women, Abbie Green and Lucy Rice, a man who called himself "Quaker," and several businessmen and farmers who had either moved to Richmond shortly before the war began or had strong ties to the Union. She had contact with at least one Union sympathizer in Confederate headquarters, and she had a list of men she could hire as guides if the need arose as well.

Union requests for information were brought into Richmond by one of two ways. Sometimes Union agents slipped into the capital at night to see Van Lew personally. She met them in a variety of locations, including her own home. If she traveled anywhere in the city, she donned a worn calico bonnet and old work clothes to make her look like a poor farm hand, and she stuffed her cheeks with cotton to alter her facial features.

Elizabeth usually rode a horse to these meetings, which were often held at night. In the beginning of the war, a farm hand on a horse was not an unusual sight in the South, and she would not have attracted much attention. But as the war dragged on, soldiers seized horses from civilians whenever an army needed mounts. Owners could object to this procedure, but few individuals could persuade Confederate soldiers that they needed horses more than the army did. As a result, fewer horses were seen on the streets of Richmond, and eventually civilians on horseback risked notice, especially near the end of the war. Even so, Elizabeth boldly mounted her steed and headed off into the night to deliver information.

While Elizabeth made no mention of being stopped on her late-night deliveries, she did record her struggle to keep her horse out of Confederate hands. According to her papers, several neighbors, who thought Elizabeth might be a spy, often watched her activities. When they discovered that she had a horse at the very time that mounts were being rounded up all over Richmond, the neighbors marched into Confederate headquarters, where they reported their discovery with great enthusiasm. The men at headquarters promised to send soldiers to Van Lew's home to check on the matter as quickly as possible.

Elizabeth learned about the soldiers' proposed visit—probably from her spy in Confederate headquarters—and she immediately hid her horse in the smokehouse. When soldiers questioned Van Lew about her neighbors' report, Elizabeth looked the men in the eye and told them that the neighbors were wrong. The soldiers asked for permission to examine the grounds anyway, and Van Lew agreed to a search. When the men checked the carriage house and found no animals, they assumed that she was telling the truth.

After the neighbors learned that no horse had been found at Van Lew's home, they insisted that the soldiers conduct another search. Officials agreed to do so, and the soldiers once again set out for Elizabeth's home. This time Elizabeth had only minutes to make preparations, but this didn't stop her from saving her mount. She told her servants to spread hay on the floor of the library while she went to the smokehouse. A few seconds before Confederate soldiers arrived, Elizabeth calmly led her stallion into the house and up the stairs to the second floor, where, needless to say, no soldier would ever think of looking for a horse.

How long her horse remained in the house isn't clear. But while he was there, Elizabeth had nothing but praise for him, even though he ate the backs of several books. She said, "He accepted his position and behaved as though he thoroughly understood matters, never stamping loud[ly] enough to be heard nor neighing. [He was] a good, loyal horse."

Most Union requests for information, though, were left in writing at the farm, and servants smuggled them into Richmond, usually nestled among the eggs. A servant would blow out the yolk and white of an egg, and slip the message into the empty shell. The eggshell was hidden among a dozen or more eggs and carried to the Van Lew mansion.

All papers, whether coming or going, were kept in one of two places in Elizabeth's home. During the day, they were hidden inside a hollow statue of a lion that stood on one of the parlor's mantels. At night, Elizabeth put the papers on her bedside stand, so she could burn the materials at a moment's notice.

In the beginning of the war, Elizabeth sent her messages to General George Henry Sharpe, the Chief of the United States Army's Bureau of Military Intelligence. Her letters describing events in Richmond before Virginia seceded and her reputation for helping Union prisoners of war, especially Congressmen Huson and Ely, should have established Van Lew as a reliable source. Nevertheless, her early information wasn't taken seriously, since few generals believed that a woman could understand war maneuvers. Also, she wasn't part of the North's regular espionage system and had no training as a spy. Ironically, Van Lew outlasted several spies who were capable, well-trained specialists in the espionage business.

Eventually the quality of her information made Elizabeth a believable source, and General Sharpe became one of her greatest admirers. He called her "one of the shrewdest and smartest women of the present age."

Later Elizabeth sent most of her information to General Benjamin Butler, and during the last year of the war, her messages were delivered to General Ulysses S. Grant's tent on the battlefield as he fought his way to Richmond. Grant, too, was impressed with Elizabeth's work, and he credited her with "sending the most valuable information received from Richmond during the war." Little did these generals know at the time how many different tasks Van Lew had to perform to get this valuable information—including eventually playing the part of a crazy woman.

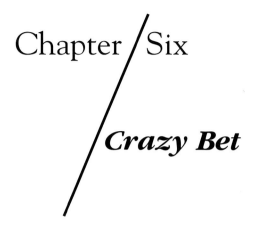

Chapter / Six

Crazy Bet

From the spring of 1861 until early 1862, many Southerners believed that they would win the war. They thought—and Northerners feared—that the Confederacy's most important European trading partner, Great Britain, would enter the conflict on the South's side, and they knew this would greatly increase their chances of winning. Southerners were convinced that Britain needed the South's cotton for its textile mills, and they believed the British would challenge the Union's naval block-ade—an act that would lead to war—to get the cotton.

Also, in 1861 the Confederacy had proved to be a strong military force. Victories at places such as Bull Run made Southern soldiers very confi-dent, and they pointed to their outstanding military leaders. Who in the North, they wondered, could possibly equal Robert E. Lee?

However, by the spring of 1862, many Southerners were no longer certain of victory. They now doubted that Britain would support the Confederacy. The British had found new sources of cotton in places like Egypt, and they no longer needed the South's supply. In addition, Britain desperately needed the Union's wheat. Because of large crop failures, the British had purchased some grain early in the war. They continued to increase their orders as the war dragged on, and by early 1863, Britain purchased more than 40 percent of all its wheat from the North. In short, Britain needed the Union's produce more than it needed the Confederacy's cotton.

Even more threatening for the South was the fact that the Confederacy was about to lose many of its soldiers in the spring of 1862. Volunteers who had enlisted with local and state militias when war broke out agreed to fight for only one year. So in April 1862, the South was forced to find replacements. But doing this was not easy. Early enthusiasm for fighting had given way to reality when news of horrible losses at the front were reported. For example, more than 23,000 men, 10,000 of them Southerners, had died recently in the battle at Shiloh, Tennessee. Furthermore, many of the men signing up in 1862 had little or no military training. The most experienced men had been the first to volunteer.

When Confederate leaders could not raise enough replacements, they decided to draft men. All males between the ages of eighteen and thirty-five were ordered to sign up for military duty. This was the first draft in American history—the North would follow with a similar law a year later—and it was not well received. Many believed that a democracy did not have the right to force men to fight. After a number of exemptions were announced which favored wealthy slaveowners over poor men, the law was even less popular. Many men now refused to register or failed to show up when ordered to join a unit.

As a result, the Confederacy lacked the numbers it needed to defend its borders. By the spring of 1862, Confederate military units began to falter. One part of the Union's army was now able to push southward along the Mississippi River while another successfully invaded New Orleans. The naval blockade along the eastern seaboard was getting tighter and tighter, and Union general McClellan was so close to Richmond that Elizabeth could hear the cannon from her home.

By mid-June many in Richmond feared that the capital would fall. Mobs flocked to Winder's office to get passes to allow them to head south. Some were so eager to leave that they didn't bother with passes—they paid an undertaker to smuggle them out of the city in coffins. The Confederacy's treasury was packed and ready to be sent to Columbia, South Carolina, where a new capital would be established if necessary, and the Confederate Congress had disbanded for the time being.

Elizabeth was among those who believed that the capital was about to be taken, and she made plans for the grand event. First of all, she prepared a room in her mansion, complete with new curtains, for General McClellan, hoping he would be her guest after Richmond surrendered. Then she made arrangements to see the last battle.

When Union forces finally advanced to within striking distance, she headed out of town to meet with other loyalists in the area. As she raced along in her carriage, she noted action everywhere as soldiers prepared to fight. "Men riding and leading horses at full speed," she wrote, "the rattling of their gear . . . the dust, the cannons in the fields, the ambulances, [and] the long line of infantry . . . waiting their orders." She was swept up by the action she saw, which, she said, "was more thrilling than I could conceive."

Shortly afterward, she arrived at the site selected by the Unionists for their viewing spot. When the artillery began to roar, the loyalists sought shelter in a nearby house. "The windows rattled and the flash of the bursting shells could be seen," Elizabeth wrote that night. "The rapid succession of the guns was wonderful. . . . I realized the bright rush of life; the hurry of death on the battlefield."

Confederate forces couldn't stop the Union in the west, but to Elizabeth's sorrow, they did stop Northern advances against Richmond. Just as Confederate forces were about to break, Robert E. Lee took to the field and made a personal appeal to his men to hold the line. His bravery and the men's loyalty to Lee reunited the Confederates, and they put up a courageous defense of Richmond. The fight for the capital lasted seven days, and more than 23,000 Southern soldiers died before the North withdrew its troops.

As cart after cart rumbled into Richmond carrying dead and dying soldiers—so many that the smell of decaying corpses and festering wounds hung over the city, according to Elizabeth—Richmonders began to look for someone to blame for the South's awful losses. Why, they wondered, had everything turned against the South? Why was the enemy suddenly so much better prepared than before? The answers to those questions were simple, some Richmonders said. We have spies among us.

From late 1861 until the end of the war, the South was convinced, correctly, that the Union had many spies in the Confederacy. Richmond newspaper editorials complained that details of battles and other events that should have been known only to a handful of generals in the South were actually appearing in articles in Northern papers. How, they asked, could such information have gotten to the North if informers hadn't passed it on? More important, how could the South hope to win with spies everywhere? Winder's men then added rounding up Union agents to their long list of things to do.

To make it easier to arrest these suspects, the Confederate government suspended the writ of habeas corpus in 1862. This gave the police the power to arrest anyone they thought was guilty of spying, without having to present proof to a judge to get a warrant. Suspending the writ infuriated many Southerners, including the Confederacy's vice president, Alexander Stephens, who argued that doing away with such a basic protection endangered every citizen, giving Winder, and others like him throughout the South, too much power.

Suspending the writ also frightened spies. From now on, rumors could be enough to land them in jail. A number of notices detailing arrests of informers appeared in Richmond newspapers as early as January 1862. Few, however, got more attention than the capture of Timothy Webster. Webster was part of Alan Pinkerton's Secret Service, one of the North's most prestigious intelligence organizations. He had made quite a name for himself when he unearthed a plot to kill Abraham Lincoln as the new president traveled to Washington for his inauguration, and in January 1862, Webster was sent to Richmond to work with several other Pinkerton agents in the capital.

When Webster failed to contact his headquarters after arriving in Richmond, two agents were sent to find him. They eventually located him in a hotel, where he lay seriously ill. The agents, who had failed to disguise themselves well, were recognized by some of Winder's men and were promptly arrested. Under intense questioning, the men betrayed Webster to save their lives.

Webster was arrested shortly afterward and

put on trial for espionage. At his trial, which ended on April 22, 1862, he was found guilty and sentenced to death. Seven days later, he was taken from his cell to a wooden platform, where a noose had been prepared. The rope was slipped over his head, and the trap door beneath him was sprung. But, suddenly, the rope snapped and a nearly dead Webster had to be hanged a second time.

Elizabeth followed Webster's arrest and trial quite carefully, and his death had a chilling effect on her, for she knew that some of Winder's men believed she was a spy. But few of the men were willing to throw a woman into jail without cause, especially a woman with Van Lew's spunk and social standing. So they set out to find proof.

Now Van Lew was routinely followed and watched. She wrote, "I have turned to speak to a friend and found a detective at my elbow. Strange faces would sometimes be seen peeping around the columns and pillars of the back portico."

When neighbors told Winder's men that they had seen strange people lurking about Van Lew's home—Union agents, in their opinion—Winder's men searched her home for messages. But Elizabeth hid her information so well that the detectives left empty-handed time after time. It's also believed that Van Lew often knew when her house was going to be checked. This is possible, since her agent in the Confederacy's office could have tipped her off.

Even though the detectives found nothing in Van Lew's home, they returned often, hoping that Elizabeth eventually would give herself away. She found the regular checks so annoying that she finally went to Winder to demand that they stop. Apparently her voice was as strong as her convictions, and she lectured Winder loudly enough for all to hear, later recording the scene in her journal. "Sir," she shouted, "your ordering your underling officers to search my home for evidence to convict me in league with the enemy is beneath the conduct of an officer and a gentleman!"

Winder didn't dare reply, but he did reconsider his actions. For a while, the house checks were halted. Besides, there were other ways to catch a spy.

The city's population increased dramatically during the war, growing from about 30,000 in 1861 to 120,000 people by the end of 1864. Most came looking for jobs in the uniform and munitions plants that mushroomed at that time.

There weren't enough hotels to house all the newcomers, or resources available to build homes, so most citizens agreed to rent out a room or two in their homes. Not only did this help with the housing situation, but it also brought in badly needed money for the home owners. Food prices were so high that some poor women actually broke into a bakery to steal bread because they could not afford to buy it. And it's no wonder bread was expensive. During the war, a barrel of flour eventually cost $1,250. Even though this sum was in inflated Confederate dollars, it was still more than many people could afford to pay.

Like other Richmonders, the Van Lews took in boarders. One of these, a young woman, received a note from Winder shortly after she moved in with Elizabeth and her mother. He asked her to come into his office and tell him all she knew about the Van Lews. The young woman reported to Winder, all right, but she made it clear that she knew nothing about spying, and she warned Elizabeth about Winder's suspicions.

When that tactic failed, Winder sent one of his own men to rent a room at the Van Lews' mansion. But from the moment the young man arrived at the door, Elizabeth felt uneasy about him. Although she had a room to rent, she sent him away. He returned later to try to get her to change her mind, but Elizabeth refused to budge. And a few days later, when she saw the man walking the streets of

Richmond with some of Winder's men, she knew her instinct had been right.

Desperate for some relief from Winder's suspicions, Van Lew then decided to take a risky step. Lieutenant David H. Todd was being replaced as commandant at one of the prisons by Lieutenant George C. Gibbs, who was about to move into the city. Elizabeth offered to rent rooms to Gibbs and his wife, hoping that, with a Confederate officer under her roof, house checks would stop and suspicions would fade away. On the other hand, with an officer coming and going regularly, Elizabeth had to be even more cautious than before, and she knew that one false step now would be fatal. Gibbs and his wife moved in for a short time, and while they were there, Winder did leave Elizabeth alone.

But the period of calm was short, and the strain of avoiding arrest was clearly beginning to take its toll on Elizabeth. Richmonders had long considered her peculiar because she was different—single, outspoken, and a Northern supporter. Day after day Richmond newspapers carried articles and editorials about how awful Northerners were, and eventually her neighbors wondered how any sane person actually could continue to support such barbarians. Then Van Lew began to show signs of stress, repeated glances over her shoulder, which made her look paranoid, and increased loud, emotional outbursts, which ladies never displayed in polite society. As these signs increased, Richmonders changed their verdict. Elizabeth was more than peculiar—she was crazy.

Van Lew decided to build on this impression, since she knew that she would be considered less of a threat if she appeared unbalanced. From time to time, she began to wear old, mismatched clothing. She would deliberately mess up her hair and don a ragged bonnet before appearing in public. Richmonders stared at her, wondering what had become of the Van Lew they knew, a pretty woman who took great pride in her appearance. Elizabeth would also talk to herself or sing as she strolled along the city's streets.

Her new role was a painful one to play, and it took great determination to carry it off. Adults laughed as she passed by, ridiculing her appearance and strange behavior, and children followed her about town, taunting her, "There goes Crazy Bet!" Meanwhile, this "crazy" woman continued to help the Union by feeding prisoners, carrying messages, and even aiding in some daring prison escapes.

Chapter / Seven

Escape!

Elizabeth had decided early on to help Union prisoners escape any way she could. She would provide a hiding place in the city and, when necessary, guides to lead them back to their units in the North. Although the date when Elizabeth began to deliberately spy for the Union isn't clear, it is certain that she began to make her first prison escape plan in November 1861.

Five months before, on June 2, 1861, Union forces captured the *Savannah*, a Southern ship whose crew members claimed to be privateers. Privateers were nonmilitary men who held letters of marque and reprisal, letters issued by governments during wartime that gave their citizens permission to capture any enemy ships, even unarmed merchant vessels. If caught, privateers could show their papers and expect to be treated as prisoners of war. Privateering had a long history, and it was a very common practice during America's Revolutionary War. In fact, colonial privateers captured many British ships loaded with arms and ammunition, and they were an important source of supplies for General Washington's army.

Like the colonists in the Revolutionary War, the Confederacy had no navy with which to fight, so to harass the enemy, President Jefferson Davis decided to start a private navy by authorizing privateering. In May 1861, his government began to issue letters of marque and reprisal. When Southerners learned that privateers would be able to keep the vast majority of any cargo they took and that a bounty was offered for every enemy warship seized as well as for every prisoner taken, many applied for the letters.

But even though privateering had been around for a long time, by 1861 many countries considered privateers little more than pirates. The United States was among these countries, and President Lincoln insisted that any privateers caught by the North's navy be tried for piracy, and if found guilty, hanged.

Therefore, when the *Savannah* was captured after attacking a Northern merchant ship loaded with sugar, the Confederacy anxiously watched to see how its crew would be treated. After Lincoln announced that crew members would be tried, just as he had said they would be, Davis protested strongly. But in spite of this protest, the trial proceeded as planned. The jury, however, was unable to reach a decision, and a mistrial was declared. A new trial was set for October.

Meanwhile, another privateer ship, the *Jefferson Davis*, was captured after it had seized two Northern ships carrying expensive cargoes. Northern ship owners and merchants demanded that this crew also be tried. "Make an example of the men!" merchants shouted. "If you don't, every person in the South who owns a boat will become a privateer!" The crew members were charged, tried, found guilty, and scheduled to hang.

Jefferson Davis was outraged. He threatened to retaliate if any of the privateers were harmed, and he told Winder to select fifteen Union prisoners to be executed if the North did indeed hang the privateers.

On November 10, Winder began the process of selection. He chose from among the highest ranking officers captured at the Battle of Bull Run. The name of each officer was written on a separate slip of paper and placed in a container in Winder's

Libby Prison, 1863

office. Winder then drew out fifteen slips, one for each privateer held. He selected six colonels, six lieutenant colonels, and three captains.

Shortly afterward, Winder's men went to Libby Prison, where most of the officers were held, and called out the names of the officers chosen to die. From this point on, these men were treated exactly as the privateers had been, as common criminals, and they were taken from Libby Prison and held in Richmond's city jail. Davis passed their names to the North, forbid their families to have any contact with them, and waited to see what the Union would do.

As soon as the men were moved to the jail, Elizabeth got a pass from Winder to visit the officers. Besides trying to give comfort, she smuggled in paper and pens so the men could write letters of farewell to their families. She mailed the letters for them and acted as a go-between for the prisoners and their families, receiving letters in her name to the prisoners from their families.

While visiting the men, Van Lew developed a special friendship with Colonel Paul Revere, a descendant of the Revolutionary War hero. As the date for the privateers' execution approached, both Van Lew and Revere doubted that the Union would back down.

So the two organized a daring escape. Although Elizabeth didn't record the plan, it's most likely that Revere hoped to bribe a guard, since he received large sums of money both from his family and from Elizabeth while in jail, and bribing guards was not uncommon in Richmond. Van Lew also made ready a secret room in her home that was located under the spot where the flat roof of the porch joined the sloping roof above the house. The entry to this long, narrow room was hidden behind a chest in the upstairs hallway. Revere planned to stay there until it was safe to make a dash to the Union's lines.

Meanwhile, great pressure was put on the Union by both the prisoners' families and leaders in foreign countries, calling for a halt to the executions. Great Britain was especially critical of

The secret porch attic in the Van Lew home

Lincoln's stand, and since the North was worried about Britain's joining the Confederacy at this point in the war, Lincoln was not eager to upset the British. Also, the Union by then had made the point that privateering was a very dangerous business, and few believed the South would continue to support the practice any longer. As a result, the privateers were not hanged, and the Union prisoners chosen to die were returned to Libby Prison.

Revere abandoned his plan to escape, hoping, correctly, that he might be sent home in a prisoner exchange. He died two years later in the battle of Gettysburg. Elizabeth's aid was never forgotten by his family, though, and they rewarded Van Lew's kindness many years later, when she was in great need.

Revere wasn't the only prisoner to think about escaping. As the number of prisoners increased—by 1863, there were more than 10,000 prisoners in Richmond—and their living conditions worsened daily, soldiers were willing to risk being shot in an attempted escape rather than remain locked up. Newspapers of the day mention numerous failed attempts by prisoners to bribe guards and to cut holes in walls to crawl through, as well as some successful breakouts.

Word spread throughout the prisons that anyone who managed to escape could expect help from Van Lew. Because her mansion was only a short distance away from the prisons, it was a convenient hideout, and prisoners did turn to her for help. In fact, Union general Sharpe credited her with helping many Northern soldiers to get back to their units.

Although Elizabeth probably helped one or two men at a time, she was equipped to house many more, and in early 1864 she prepared for the biggest breakout to date. In January, Van Lew was told that a tunnel had been started at Libby Prison, and a mass exodus was planned. In addition to getting the secret room ready, Van Lew covered the windows in one of the parlors with blankets and waited for the escapees to arrive.

Then on February 8, she received a devastating message from her brother. He had been drafted. Until then, John had been exempt from the draft because of his age and poor health. But as the pool of available soldiers became smaller and smaller during the war, men who had once been excused from the army were being called on to serve. John, now thirty-eight years old, was suddenly declared fit to fight. Although not as active as Elizabeth was, John, too, was an ardent Union supporter. To avoid fighting for the Confederacy, he decided to desert and try to get to the Union's lines. If possible, he wanted to see Elizabeth before heading north.

As soon as it was dark, Elizabeth donned a disguise and went to the home outside the city where John was being hidden, one of her spy ring's safe houses. She feared for her brother's safety. If caught, John would either be taken to prison, a death sentence for a man in poor health, or shot for deserting. On the other hand, if he made it to the Union's lines, she would not see him for a long time. In either case, they would be parted, and her feelings were summed up in one word in her scrapbook. She wrote "agony" across John's draft notice.

In the morning, just before she was about to return to Richmond, one of her servants arrived with news that the expected breakout from Libby Prison had taken place the night before. Confederate soldiers were everywhere, the servant reported, looking for the prisoners. Elizabeth quickly realized that there was little chance now that John could get away.

She decided to return to Richmond immediately. She promised John that she would try to talk Winder into getting an exemption for him. Flattery had worked so far, she argued; maybe it could do the trick one more time. Besides, she added, it was John's only chance now to avoid prison or worse. Meanwhile, he had to remain in hiding.

As soon as Elizabeth reached her home, servants filled her in on the escape. When roll call was taken at Libby Prison on the morning of February 9, the guards discovered that 109 prisoners were missing. That's when the alarm bells were rung and citizens and soldiers alike began to look for the prisoners. The servants also told Elizabeth that a number of men had appeared at the side door the night before, begging to enter. The servants were afraid that the men were really Confederate agents trying to trick them, and they turned the men away. Now the servants were filled with remorse.

Shortly afterward, Van Lew received word that prisoners had been hidden in several homes. The men, after crawling out of the tunnel—a feat that was slowed down when a heavy prisoner got stuck in the narrow passage and had to be pulled through—were met by Mrs. Abbie Green, who took them to various hiding spots. When the escapees were turned away from the Van Lew home, their guide took them to another shelter.

The prisoners hoped to make their way to Union lines as soon as it was practical to do so. Meanwhile, the soldiers wanted Elizabeth to send a message to Union generals, asking them to give interviews to various newspapers announcing that some escapees had reached safety. It was hoped that this lie would encourage Confederates to call off the search soon and would thus shorten the time prisoners had to remain in hiding.

A few days later, one of the escaped prisoners asked to see Van Lew. Mrs. Lucy Rice, who lived in the home where four Union soldiers were hiding, immediately contacted Elizabeth, and under cover of dark, Elizabeth went to see the men. She met with Colonel Abel D. Streight, the leader of the escape, Major Bedan McDonald, who did most of the tunneling work, and two others whom she did not identify in her journal.

Elizabeth was very impressed with the men, and they talked freely about several issues. She informed Streight that the Confederates were especially eager to recapture him, for there were many rumors about his once leading a black regiment. Streight, in high spirits, replied that he was aware of the false rumors, but he was still very optimistic about getting through Confederate lines. Major McDonald then described how the tunnel had been made, and he showed Elizabeth the chisel he had used to chop a hole through the foundation of Libby Prison. Elizabeth wrote that they shared a little laughing as they talked about the escape, and the evening went quickly.

As Van Lew left the men, she wished them an emotional farewell. She wrote, "I said good-by with the most fervent God bless you in my heart toward all of them." It was far too dangerous for Elizabeth to make the trip again, and it was the last time that she saw these men, although Mrs. Rice (who went North a few months later, along with Mrs. Green, to avoid arrest) kept her posted on their whereabouts.

Of the 109 men who escaped, 65 prisoners were recaptured, but Streight and McDonald were not among them. Shortly after Streight reached safety at Fortress Monroe on February 24, he was interviewed by a newspaper reporter from the *New York Herald*, and the article was reprinted in the *Washington Chronicle* five days later.

When the editor at the *Richmond Examiner* received copies of the interview, he was aghast. Streight claimed that he had been secreted only a few miles from Richmond for days without being discovered, and when the prisoners finally left the area, they carried arms and six days of rations, real luxuries in a town where guns and food were very scarce.

The editor at the *Examiner* found the interview "interesting" because it proved that there were many Union men—he should have said women, as well—at large in Richmond. "What more can we expect," the editor asked, "if our authorities are not more vigilant?" He had only a few days to wonder about coming events, for one of the most bizarre incidents of the war, which would further expose and endanger the Unionists in Richmond, was about to take place.

Chapter / Eight

/ Reburying the Dead

Provost Marshal Winder believed that 10,000 prisoners in Richmond presented a security threat to the capital. He feared that even a few escapees could ignite the armory, the Confederacy's main source of guns, or worse yet, storm the munitions factory, arm themselves, and attack government officials.

Winder also believed that the number of prisoners would increase dramatically during the coming months, for by 1864, prisoner-of-war exchanges had been halted. Union generals opposed exchanges in order to keep as many potential Confederate soldiers off the battlefield as possible. Although this meant that the North also would have many soldiers in prison, the Union had a much larger population from which to draw troops.

An increase in the number of prisoners meant more overcrowding in the prisons, and Winder feared that the Yankees might riot as a result. Thousands might escape then, and Winder really worried about the harm that number might do. In addition, he was well aware that so many prisoners in one location so close to the Union's border provided a tempting target. Northern raiders might decide to rush in and free the prisoners without bothering with an exchange. So while Colonel Streight and Major McDonald were planning their escape in January 1864, Confederate officials were making plans to move Richmond's prisoners to Georgia.

Even though Winder tried to keep these plans a secret so that the Union wouldn't try a last-minute raid to free the prisoners, Elizabeth learned that the men were to be sent south, and she contacted General Butler's Union headquarters at Fortress Monroe. She knew that a number of Confederate troops usually assigned to the Richmond area were away at the moment. As a result, Van Lew believed that Richmond was so poorly defended just then that raiders could charge in, free the prisoners, and get them back to Union lines without too much trouble.

Although Elizabeth asked to have all her correspondence returned to her at the end of the war, the clerk who emptied Van Lew's file overlooked one message. It is the message, originally in cipher, that Van Lew sent to Butler suggesting a raid on Richmond. She said:

> *Dear Sir,*
>
> *It is intended to remove to Georgia all the federal prisoners; butchers and bakers to go at once. They are already notified and selected. Quaker [one of Van Lew's agents] knows this to be true. Are building batteries on the Danville road. . . . No attempt should be made with less than 30,000 cavalry, from 10,000 to 15,000 to support them, amounting in all to 40,000 to 45,000 troops. Do not underrate their strength and desperation. Forces could probably be called into action in from five to ten days; 25,000, mostly artillery. Hoke's and Kemper's brigades gone to North Carolina; Pickett's in or about Petersburg. Three regiments of cavalry disbanded by General Lee for want of horses.*

Shortly after Butler received this information, he wrote to the secretary of war, Edwin Stanton. Butler encouraged Stanton to send in the cavalry to free the prisoners, advice the secretary followed.

Stanton contacted General Judson Kilpatrick and Colonel Ulric Dahlgren and told them to plan a secret raid on Richmond. Unfortunately for Kilpatrick and Dahlgren, some men in their units talked about their exciting assignment, and word of their raid became common knowledge in Washington.

The Confederates had a number of spies in the Union's capital, and they warned Richmond officials about a possible attack. As soon as Winder received the warning, he alerted the home guard and placed barrels of gunpowder around the prisons. He told the captives that he would ignite the barrels if anyone attempted to break out when the cavalry arrived, and he assured the prisoners that the explosions would kill most of them.

On February 28, Kilpatrick and Dahlgren led 4,000 men, a number far short of the 40,000 soldiers Van Lew had suggested, toward Richmond. At the same time, another 2,000 Union soldiers—who would soon be joined by other troops—left Washington and marched toward Charlottesville to create a diversion.

On the night of February 28–29, Dahlgren and Kilpatrick parted, and Dahlgren and his 300 raiders began to make their way to the James River along back roads and unmarked trails. These men planned to ride into Richmond from the south and free the prisoners on Belle Isle. Kilpatrick was supposed to enter the capital from the north. After the two raiding parties met in Richmond, they hoped to free the rest of the prisoners and rush toward Butler—and safety!—at Fortress Monroe.

On March 1, Dahlgren started to run into difficulties. His guide either couldn't or wouldn't find the ford on the James River, one of the few spots where it was safe to cross. Legend has it that Dahlgren suspected that his guide was in the pay of the Confederates, and the Colonel paused just long enough to hang him.

It was very risky to go on without a guide, but Dahlgren refused to give up on the raid, and he continued to push toward Richmond on March 2. Late in the afternoon, the colonel encountered his first sniper fire from home guards, and the shooting became more intense as the raiders neared the capital. Clearly the countryside had been warned that the cavalry was coming, and Dahlgren began to worry about what awaited his men in Richmond. When Dahlgren was within five miles of the capital, he encountered so much resistance that he had little choice but to call a retreat. Kilpatrick, coming from the north, also was forced to turn back.

Colonel Ulric Dahlgren

As the discouraged men started toward Washington, it began to rain. They didn't dare take time to find shelter to wait out the downpour, since the enemy's forces were growing by the minute. Instead, the very wet, thoroughly chilled cavalry slogged on through the mud as fast as they could.

Around midnight, the men rode into an ambush, and gunfire rang out all around them. Dahlgren and thirty-one of his men were killed immediately. The other raiders had little choice but to surrender, and they did so shortly after their leader's death. They were marched off to jail, and Dahlgren was left, face down in the mud, for the burial crew.

News about the capture of the raiders spread rapidly, and local citizens, as well as some soldiers in the area, rode out to see the ambush site the next morning. Before the burial crew arrived, Dahlgren's orders were taken from his body for examination, and the little finger on his left hand was cut off so a diamond ring could be removed. An artificial limb that he wore on his right leg below the knee was also removed, as were his gold watch and coat. They were taken to Richmond and put on display. When the burial crew finally arrived, they wrapped what was left of Dahlgren in a blanket, placed him in a wooden coffin, and buried him where he had died, in a spot Elizabeth described as a "slashy mud hole."

At first, Richmonders begrudgingly admired the Union raiders for their brave rescue attempt. But when the newspapers published the papers supposedly found on Dahlgren, admiration quickly turned to outrage. These papers ordered Dahlgren to burn Richmond to the ground and to kill Jefferson Davis. Although some sources think the orders were forged by Confederate officials to make

Southerners fighting mad, the city's newspapers believed them to be authentic. One editor called Ulric Dahlgren "Ulric the Hun" and told readers that Dahlgren's name had been added to the scroll of infamy, a list of history's worst villains.

Just before Jefferson Davis learned about Dahlgren's papers, he had ordered grave diggers to bring the raider's body to Richmond for a more fitting burial. It was too late to stop the order, and the work crew brought the corpse to the capital on March 6, about the same time that Richmonders learned of the infamous orders. Feelings were running pretty high by then, and the decision to provide a fitting burial was scrapped. Instead, Dahlgren's body was put on display, so that all could see what this evil person really looked like, and thousands took the opportunity to do so. Then, ignoring requests for the body from Dahlgren's family, Confederates secretly buried the colonel in an unmarked site. Officials wanted to be certain that no one ever shed a tear of sympathy over the raider's remains.

Elizabeth and her agents had been appalled by the lack of respect shown to Dahlgren. She wrote, "The heart of every loyal person was stirred to its depths by the outrages committed upon his inanimate body." There had been little any of them could do, but as soon as Dahlgren was buried for the second time, Van Lew's agents began to look for his grave. Unknown to the burial crew, there was a witness to Dahlgren's second burial, and agent F. W. E. Lohmann finally found the man. Meanwhile Elizabeth made plans to steal the body, give it a decent burial, and when the war was over, send the casket to Dahlgren's family.

Besides Van Lew and the witness to the burial, five men and two women were involved in this scheme. F. W. E. Lohmann and his brother John agreed to open the grave and take the body. M. M. Lipscomb, a Richmond undertaker, said he also would help to remove the casket and to furnish a metallic coffin, a major contribution since there were only two left in Richmond at the time. William Rowley volunteered to take the coffin to a new grave, and Robert Orrick agreed to bury the body on his farm, ten miles north of Richmond. Two women who worked for Orrick offered to help him bury Dahlgren.

On the night of April 6, the Lohmanns and Lipscomb plus the person who had seen the burial, an unnamed black man, headed to Oakwood Cemetery in an old wooden wagon. The man showed the Unionists where the grave was and then held the lantern—offering a prayer now and then—as the men dug away, working as quickly as possible to unearth the casket. Once they reached the coffin, they pried it open, unwrapped the body, and examined the corpse to make sure they had the right one. As soon as the men were certain that they had Dahlgren's remains, they removed the casket, filled in the grave, loaded the coffin onto the wagon, and headed for Rowley's farm.

When the wagon arrived at Rowley's, the coffin was taken to a storage shed where Van Lew met the men. The casket was pried open once again, and Elizabeth, and several Unionists who had been invited, inspected the body. Van Lew was amazed at how well preserved Dahlgren's body was, considering how long he had been buried, and she noticed only a few spots of mildew on his head. After clipping a lock of his reddish brown hair, she ordered the men to shave Dahlgren in an attempt to disguise his body.

The next morning, the Lohmann brothers and Lipscomb returned with the new casket, and Dahlgren's corpse was placed inside. The coffin was sealed with a homemade putty, since there was no more sealing compound left anywhere in Richmond, and was carried to Rowley's two-horse wagon. The men covered the coffin with two or three inches of dirt and topped the dirt with several layers of small peach trees. The trees in each layer were carefully arranged side by side, their branches and bare roots entwined. Lipscomb returned to Richmond, and the Lohmanns rode on ahead of Rowley. They planned to meet him near Orrick's farm—if he didn't get arrested by the guards at the checkpoint through which he had to pass on the outskirts of town.

Rowley knew how dangerous his situation was, yet hard as it may seem, he managed to look relaxed as he drove toward the sentries. When he finally arrived for the wagon check, this man of incredible self-control did all he could to appear calm and indifferent to a possible inspection.

A guard took one look at the pile of trees, and realizing an examination would take some time, asked Rowley to pull his wagon off to the side. But before the guard could look at Rowley's load, other wagons pulled up. Their drivers were clearly in a hurry, and Rowley graciously told the guard to check the others first.

After a wait of about fifteen minutes—a wait that must have seemed like forever to Rowley—the guard's supervisor became concerned that Rowley was being held up unnecessarily. He shouted at the guard, ordering him to check that man's wagon immediately or let him go through.

The guard returned to Rowley's wagon, and after exchanging a few pleasantries with him, studied the peach trees again. He was clearly hesitant to disturb such a neatly packed load, a factor on which the Unionists had counted. The guard then walked back to the driver's seat and studied Rowley's face for a moment. As Rowley looked the guard in the eye, the guard announced his decision, a decision Rowley repeated to Elizabeth when he reported the day's events. "I don't want to hinder you any longer. I think it all right, at any rate your honest face is guarantee enough for me—go on."

Rowley reached for the reins, and after smiling at the guard, he drove off slowly so he wouldn't raise any suspicion. He was met by the Lohmanns a few miles north of the city as planned, and the three then went to Orrick's farm. Dahlgren's remains were buried there, and one of the peach trees was planted on top of the grave to mark the site. Shortly afterward, the men returned to Richmond to give their report.

As soon as Van Lew knew the body was safe, she put the lock that she had cut of Dahlgren's hair into a locket and sent the locket and a message to General Butler. She asked the general to forward the locket to Dahlgren's family and tell them that the colonel's body was safe and that it would be sent to them at the end of the war.

Although, as Elizabeth wrote later, ". . . every true Union heart, who knew of this day's work, felt happier," Dahlgren's family had been unaware of Van Lew's plan until the message arrived. Instead, Dahlgren's father, Admiral John Dahlgren, had been pleading, unsuccessfully, with Confederate officials to send his son's remains home. Finally, after personally contacting President Davis, Admiral Dahlgren secured a promise from Davis that the coffin would be sent home, much to everyone's surprise.

Only a few days after Lipscomb and the Lohmann brothers had taken the casket from Oakwood Cemetery, the Confederates who had originally buried Dahlgren were told to remove the coffin from the secret grave. The men went to the cemetery and dug for quite a while before reaching the incredible conclusion that the grave was empty. They immediately reported the coffin's disappearance to their commanding officer, who was dumbfounded.

Most Richmonders also were dumbfounded when they learned that Dahlgren's body was missing. Why, they wondered, would anyone take a corpse? One of Winder's men, Colonel

McCubbin, shared his theory with Richmonders, and it soon became the most accepted solution to the mystery. McCubbin told the *Richmond Dispatch* that "certain citizens, indignant over the orders found on Colonel Dahlgren's body, have found the grave, taken the body and chopped it into pieces."

It must have been hard for Van Lew, Rowley, and the rest to keep straight faces when they heard McCubbin's theory. Nevertheless, they concealed the truth well. What really happened wasn't told until the war ended, when Dahlgren's body was dug up one more time and sent home to its final resting place in Philadelphia.

William S. Rowley

Illiam S. Rowley, like Elizabeth Van Lew, had strong ties to the North. Rowley, his wife, and his three sons were all natives of New York, and the Rowleys had lived on their farm near Richmond for only two years before the war broke out.

Since he was a Dunkard, a member of a religious group that opposes war, and he was forty-five years old when the war started, the Confederates did not draft Rowley. However, he was forced to serve on a Southern ambulance crew at least once, carrying wounded Confederate soldiers in his wagon to hospitals in Richmond.

His activities for the Union were quite varied. Besides helping to relocate Dahlgren's body, Rowley gathered information and sent it north, and he bought forged passes that escapees or Union agents could use to get out of Richmond. In addition, Rowley made his home available to the Unionists. Agents from the North met there with members of Van Lew's spy ring. Sometimes Elizabeth herself went there when she felt it was too dangerous for an agent to come to her house. It was at Rowley's farm that Van Lew received her invisible ink and instructions on how to use it from an agent who slipped into the Confederacy for a brief meeting with Van Lew.

Rowley's neighbors suspected him of spying for the Union, and they reported their suspicions to Winder. As a result, Rowley was arrested twice. But the neighbors were unable to provide any proof, and Winder's men decided to release the calm, quiet suspect after questioning.

After the war, Rowley sold his old home and bought a larger farm near Richmond.

Chapter / Nine

Richmond Falls

Even though Van Lew had seen lots of action and encountered incredible danger during the first years of the war, in early 1865, only a few months before peace would be declared, Elizabeth was facing her most dangerous situation. By then she was sending a steady stream of military information to General Grant, and the sheer number of messages greatly increased her chances of getting caught. In February the Union, hungry for even more intelligence, had accepted the help of R. W. Pole, the Englishman who almost destroyed Van Lew's spy ring. Pole's clever scheme had resulted in the arrest of two of Elizabeth's agents, and there was always the danger that they might slip up under intense questioning and implicate her.

Also, the mood in Richmond had turned for

the worse. The city was under siege. When Grant had begun his drive to the capital, the South's last stronghold, he had encountered such fierce resistance from the Confederates that he finally decided to starve the city into submission rather than sacrifice more men on the battlefield. To do this, he had swung around Richmond, hoping to cut off all supply lines leading into the capital from the south. He was very successful, and by early March 1865, only one Southern railroad line near Petersburg was open. The siege was very effective: General Lee's men had little left with which to fight, and most Richmonders had little to eat. They then looked for someone upon whom they could take out their rage and grief as Grant made their lives more and more unbearable each day. Threats against Elizabeth increased dramatically.

Worse yet for Richmonders was the fact that Lee's forces, outnumbered by more than 70,000 men, were inadequate to break the siege or to hold on to Petersburg if the Union attacked in force. By the middle of March, the situation was so desperate that Lee was forced to consider abandoning Richmond and Petersburg before Union troops cut off his only escape route and completely encircled his men. Rumors about such plans were common in the capital, and many believed that Lee's withdrawal meant the end of the Confederacy. At the very least, it meant that Union forces finally would be able to occupy the capital, and this did little to improve the mood in the city.

In late March, just as Southerners had feared, Grant moved to cut off the one remaining railroad line servicing Richmond. Bitter fighting ensued, and on April 1, Lee sent a message to President Davis telling him that his army was moving southward, hoping to regroup with other Confederate forces in the field. He could no longer protect Richmond.

On Sunday morning, April 2, a messenger handed Davis the note from Lee while he was attending services at St. Paul's Episcopal Church. Members of the congregation were well aware of Richmond's perilous predicament, and they studied Davis's reaction carefully as he read the message. When Davis, pale and visibly shaken, rose to leave the church, few doubted that the capital was about to fall. Even so, parishioners remained in their pews until the service ended, praying for a miracle.

Early that afternoon, Davis announced that the army was abandoning Richmond. Chaos followed. People rushed about, trying to gather a few belongings for a quick getaway. Banks opened so that customers could withdraw their funds before departing, and citizens scrambled to be first in line to get money for their escape. Although soldiers tried to destroy all liquor supplies, mobs interfered and whiskey flowed freely. As a result, drunken men and women wandered about the city, looking for fights, adding to the growing confusion. Meanwhile, all the scoundrels the newspapers once complained about who had moved into Richmond during the war, looked for anything of value they might take from abandoned homes and stores.

By late afternoon, all available carts, wagons, and wheelbarrows—even Van Lew's, which her neighbors stole—were loaded with belongings and driven or pushed to the railroad depot, where Richmonders fought over the few precious spaces still available in the railroad cars. Most were already overflowing with government officials and their families or crammed full of Confederate records, documents, and a few treasure chests. Signs of fear, rage, and frustration were everywhere, and cries, curses, and shouts could be heard well past nightfall.

But not everyone could leave Richmond, or wanted to, including Van Lew. Most of these people gathered their precious belongings and tried to find a safe place for them. They knew that once the soldiers had withdrawn, there was a good chance that law and order would break down completely, and looting would become widespread. So Elizabeth spent some of her time on April 2 hiding the family's silverware, and when neighbors who had often accused Van Lew of spying asked her to hide theirs, Van Lew, who could be so strong, even hard-hearted when necessary, agreed.

Before leaving that night, Confederate troops tried to destroy anything they could not carry that might be of use to the Union. They rolled cannonballs into the river and set the armament factories on fire. More than 800,000 shells exploded over a period of five hours, and the noise and smoke added greatly to the confusion. Sparks from these fires were carried by the wind, and soon several sections of Richmond were ablaze. Those who remained in the city were shorthanded and unorganized, and they could do little to put out the flames.

Elizabeth stayed up all night, anxiously watching the fires from her home, and when daylight broke on April 3, she and a servant rode downtown to see what damage had been done. She viewed the ruins with mixed feelings. The sight of such destruction caused despair, but the fact that the city had finally been brought to its knees also

An artist's depiction of the fall of Richmond

brought satisfaction. She wrote, "Our beautiful flour mills, the largest in the world and the prize of our city, were destroyed. Square after square of stores, dwelling homes, factories, warehouses, banks, hotels, bridges all wrapped in fire—all filled the city with clouds of smoke as incense from the land for its deliverance. What a moment!"

Angry mobs were surveying the damage as well, and when Elizabeth heard shouts of "There goes Crazy Bet!" she ordered her servant to turn around. Elizabeth didn't intimidate easily, but she knew she would be risking her life if she went any farther. Besides, she had seen enough for the moment, and she had work to do at home.

Richmond in ruins

As soon as she reached her mansion, she raised a new American flag, measuring 20 feet by 9 feet, more than big enough for all to see, above her house. General Butler had obtained this flag for her, and somehow she had managed to smuggle it into Richmond. For months she had planned to have it on display to welcome the Union troops when they arrived. It was dangerous for Van Lew to do this, but no amount of personal peril was going to stop her grand gesture now.

Understandably, the flag upset Richmonders. An angry mob marched toward the Van Lew home, vowing to tear the Stars and Stripes down, and a few were prepared to burn it—and to burn the mansion to the ground.

As the mob pushed closer and closer to her back door, Elizabeth knew she could not ignore it. She also knew she could not afford to let anyone enter her home. Besides her frail mother, Elizabeth was caring for her brother's ten-year-old daughter and harboring two men who had escaped from one of the prisons. One of the escapees is thought to have been William White, one of the spies awaiting execution who had been betrayed by Pole. If so, Richmonders would have loved to get their hands on White, and they would not have looked kindly upon anyone who had helped him.

Van Lew sized up the mob, then—unarmed— stepped out onto the porch. Looking the mob leaders straight in the eye, she shouted, "Lower this flag or hurt one bit of my house and I will see that General Butler pays you back in kind . . . every one of you!" She looked at the crowd, picking out those she recognized. "I know you . . . and you!" she added as she pointed at one individual after another. None in the crowd wanted to find out if Van Lew was bluffing, especially if she knew who they were, and the mob broke up.

Federal troops began arriving in Richmond early that morning. While most rushed toward the capitol building, Grant's aide-de-camp, Colonel Parke, headed to Van Lew's mansion. Grant feared that Elizabeth might be in great danger, and Parke had been sent to protect her.

But Parke did not find Elizabeth at home. As

soon as she learned that federal troops were entering the city, Elizabeth had raced to Confederate headquarters, where Colonel Parke finally spotted her, sifting through the remaining documents, hoping to find something the Union could use. Although Confederates had burned the most important papers or taken the materials with them, Elizabeth found several historically important documents. They included a file containing papers and a booklet written by John Brown that had been taken from him when he was arrested at Harpers Ferry.

Once Union soldiers arrived, they immediately began to restore order. Some fought fires, others arrested drunks, and many stood guard throughout the city to prevent looting. President Lincoln had insisted that Richmond be offered generous surrender terms, and wagons loaded with food began to arrive within hours after the first soldiers rode into town.

President Lincoln had been staying nearby, waiting for the momentous surrender, and on April 4, he entered Richmond. He rode through town, visited Libby Prison, and toured the Confederate White House. Former black slaves, who were considered officially freed as soon as Union troops arrived, curiosity seekers, and loyalists lined the streets to see him. Van Lew made no mention in her papers of seeing Lincoln, but it's hard to imagine that she didn't join the crowds to welcome the president.

Grant did not accompany the Union troops that entered the capital on April 3. Instead, he pursued Lee as he retreated, hoping to catch him before the remaining Southern soldiers could meet and reorganize. Grant was successful, and Lee surrendered his troops on April 9. This is generally considered the end of the war, even though the last of the Confederate soldiers did not surrender until April 26.

Shortly after Lee's surrender, Grant and his wife went to Richmond, and their first stop in the city was the Van Lew mansion. Elizabeth did not record their conversation in her journal—and it must have been interesting, to say the least—but she did add Grant's calling card to her scrapbook, a reminder of one of her most memorable moments.

Richmonders were relieved by President Lincoln's generous surrender terms. He clearly did not want to punish the South, and many Confederates believed that the two parts of the nation could put the awful war behind them and live in harmony.

But on April 15, President Lincoln died from an assassin's bullet, and many Northerners believed that Southerners were responsible for his death. In fact, after his arrest, Jefferson Davis was actually accused of being involved in the plot to kill the president and his cabinet.

Powerful leaders in Congress added Lincoln's death to their list of reasons why the South should be punished, and they prepared to unleash their fury in the coming years. The new president, Andrew Johnson, along with those members of Congress who still favored Lincoln's plan for reuniting the country, were pushed aside. The new leaders, who came to be known as Radical Republicans, drew up a harsh plan for Reconstruction. Many former Confederates lost their voting rights, and Southern states were denied representation in Congress and put under military rule. As a result, the hatred many Southerners felt for the North grew even more.

Chapter / Ten

Working Woman

As soon as the fighting on the battlefields ended in 1865, Union loyalists in the South appealed to the federal government for funds. Some supporters wanted to be reimbursed for their wartime expenses, such as housing and supplying prison escapees. Others wanted a fee for duties performed. Applicants had to give written statements that explained in detail what they had done to deserve payment. They also had to provide statements from others that backed up their claims.

Only a few months after the war ended, several members of Van Lew's ring appealed for funds, and Elizabeth wrote letters on their behalf.

In doing this, she revealed her part in moving
Dahlgren's body, her efforts to help soldiers escape,
and some of her spying activities.

Although Van Lew had received some money
during the war to offset her expenses, Union generals felt she deserved much more. General Butler
recommended that $15,000 be given to Elizabeth,
and as a congressional committee debated this
request—only $5,000 was finally agreed upon, for
reasons that aren't clear—more of Van Lew's
adventures came to light.

Some Richmonders had long suspected
Elizabeth of spying, but the majority thought that
anyone of her social standing simply couldn't be a
spy. They thought spies occupied the lowest rung
on the social ladder, right next to prostitutes. In
fact, most thought female spies got their information by seducing men, and they could barely
contain their shock and disgust when rumors
about Van Lew's activities made the rounds.
Elizabeth had reached a new low in their opinion,
and they sneered when they said her name.

Besides testifying on behalf of her agents,
Elizabeth tried to aid the newly freed slaves. These
men, women, and children, almost 4 million in
total, had no money or property of their own upon
which they could live, and they had few job skills.

Projects were started by both the federal government and private organizations to educate the former slaves, and according to newspaper articles published after Elizabeth's death, she invested money in several of these programs. The *Richmond Times* called them "wild, unpractical schemes," and Elizabeth lost considerable money backing them. As a result, only a few years after the war ended, Van Lew was facing serious financial problems.

But help was not far away. General Grant was elected president in 1868, and he was well aware of Elizabeth's difficulties. Elizabeth asked for the position of postmaster of Richmond, and 15 days after Grant was inaugurated, he offered her the position. Although in the 1800s, few women worked outside their homes, both the federal and Confederate governments had hired women during the war, when men were not available to fill the positions. This practice was very controversial, but because the women's work had proven to be satisfactory, the federal government continued to hire them after the war ended. Elizabeth's appointment as postmaster, then, was not the first of its kind. But her salary, if newspaper reports can be believed, was unusual. It was claimed that she earned $4,000 a year. Few working women earned more than $1,000 a year in the 1860s. If the

$4,000 sum reported is correct, Elizabeth was given an enviable position.

People reacted to Van Lew's appointment in a variety of ways. Stories about Elizabeth's support for the Union circulated throughout the North, where she was called a heroine, and her selection as postmaster was approved by most Northerners. A *New York Times* article said, "Miss Van Lew's appointment has given highest satisfaction to the country." On the other hand, Richmonders considered the appointment an outrage. The *Richmond Enquirer*, referring to the *Times* article, reacted by printing: "Please excuse Richmond if you count that as part of the country. We are not at all pleased here. We regard the selection of a Federal spy to manage our post office as a deliberate insult to our people."

Even though Richmonders objected, Elizabeth, now 50 years old, began working at the post office on April 1, 1869. She made few changes in the office, and because she was personally backed by the president of the United States, most of her clerks resisted the temptation to harass her for her wartime activities—for a while.

Grant was reelected in 1872, and he again appointed Van Lew postmaster, but his second term was weakened by scandals. Richmonders, sensing that Grant was no longer a political power, had less fear of upsetting Elizabeth, and when the opportunity to persecute her presented itself, some clerks took advantage of it, hoping to drive her out of the post office.

Van Lew had no experience in supervising people who didn't like her, and her outrage at their lack of respect only encouraged her tormentors to continue their attacks. By 1874, after months of difficulty on the job, Van Lew wrote to Grant's secretary, telling him to "ask the president to protect me." She complained about a terrible conspiracy in her office, which she believed was led by her chief clerk, who wanted her position. Van Lew accused the clerk of starting rumors about her, calling her "irrational," "peculiar," and "a stingy old maid."

It was not unusual for women to expect men to fight their battles for them then. Elizabeth accepted this custom when it suited her, and she was never afraid to go to the most powerful person she knew for support. She even had asked President Davis for protection during the war when threats were made against her home. And when she had stared down the mob intent on tearing down her new flag, she had relied upon the knowledge that Union troops, who would back her up, were just outside Richmond. But Grant had too many problems of his own to be able to help Van Lew, and since she was only as strong as the man backing her, her situation became almost impossible.

What was striking about Elizabeth's predicament was her shock at being persecuted. She honestly didn't understand why anyone wanted to hurt her. First of all, she couldn't understand the Richmonders' deep sense of betrayal, because she believed so strongly that her support for the Union had been the right thing to do. In her eyes, the Richmonders were the traitors, so why, she wondered, was she being punished?

Second, she failed to understand society's resistance to change. By becoming a working woman— and a supervisor at that—at a time when women were expected to remain at home, Elizabeth had challenged one of society's long-standing customs. Challengers are often persecuted because people fear change. Van Lew, unfortunately, simply wasn't prepared for the harassment. It's interesting to note that many women who went to work at that time ran into similar, or even worse, situations. In the patent office in Washington, D.C., for example, some male workers lined the halls at the office and spit at female clerks when they came to work, or

An outdoor gathering of the Van Lew family shortly after Mrs. Van Lew's death. From left to right are Elizabeth's brother, John; his son, John Newton; his daughter Anna; Scorpio, a former slave; John's daughter Eliza; and Elizabeth.

made incredibly rude remarks, more shocking than anything Elizabeth reported.

Even though Van Lew couldn't understand why she was being harassed, her position in Richmond society was made very clear when her mother died in 1875. Elizabeth was unable to find six men in the whole city who would act as pallbearers at Mrs. Van Lew's funeral. She complained bitterly afterward that Richmonders snickered when they talked about the funeral. Because a number of blacks had attended the service, Richmonders referred to the funeral in the most derogatory terms, including "nigger service."

Elizabeth's brother had returned to Richmond only a few days after the capital fell. Although Elizabeth had been successful in persuading Winder to assign her brother to a local unit that was unlikely to see action when John was drafted in February 1864, her brother was ordered to the front three months later. John decided to desert again, arriving in the North in early June. His refusal to fight for the Confederacy outraged Richmonders, and he was held in contempt by the people. When he returned, he lacked the necessary funds to operate a business of his own, and no one would hire him. Elizabeth appealed to Grant for a government position for her brother, but Grant did not give John an appointment.

After Mrs. Van Lew died, John, his second wife, his two daughters, and his son temporarily moved into the Van Lew mansion, in part to try to ease the terrible pain that Elizabeth felt over her mother's death. The family members held on to each other for support, and Elizabeth's salary became the family's main source of income. This state of affairs also helps to explain why Elizabeth was so upset when she ran into problems at work; she couldn't afford to lose her job.

Nevertheless, in 1876, Grant was not renominated for president, and Elizabeth's position was in real jeopardy. As a candidate, Rutherford Hayes, the new president, had campaigned against the Radical Republicans' Reconstruction program. He had promised to appoint a Southerner as postmaster general as well, and it was commonly believed that the new president would most likely choose former Confederates as postmasters in the South.

Hayes's election, welcomed by many Southerners, marked the end of Reconstruction—few Radicals held office now—and Northerners, eager to put the bitter strife between the North and South behind them, no longer gave open support to former loyalists, even when pressured to do so. Although Grant urged Hayes to leave Van Lew in the Richmond post office, the new president refused to reappoint her. Not only was Elizabeth out of a job, but she was asked to leave her position early. To add to her pain, Richmonders taunted her about being abandoned by her Northern friends.

Her neighbors may have thought she was all alone, but Elizabeth still had a few powerful friends. Although President Hayes would not reappoint her as postmaster in 1876, even after she attempted to see him personally, she continued to seek a government position in Richmond, applying for postmaster again after the election of 1880 when James Garfield became president-elect. Finally, she gave up on the idea of working in Richmond, and in 1883, she accepted a clerking job in the post office department in Washington.

Elizabeth was greatly relieved to find work, but her new job created as many problems as it solved. She now had a steady income, but her salary was significantly lower than it had been in Richmond, only $1,200 a year, and it had to go further than before. Besides maintaining her mansion in Richmond, she had to rent an apartment in Washington.

In addition, Van Lew ran into problems at the office. She claimed that she was a devoted employee, while others insisted that she came late, left early, and often missed work because of health problems. Her supervisor, who watched her carefully, was a Southerner, and Elizabeth felt that he persecuted her because of her wartime activities. Van Lew tried flattery to get him to stop his constant criticism, and when that failed, she resorted to her old trick of using food to win over the enemy. This time, instead of using custard to get a pass into Richmond's prisons, she baked cakes to end complaints. She indicated in her papers that these treats seemed to do the trick for a while, but eventually her boss began his verbal assaults again. These attacks were so sharp that even fellow workers were stunned.

Elizabeth also came under harsh criticism when she voiced her political opinions. She wrote letters to newspapers, complaining that government programs had kept the South poor. She also expressed anger that, as a woman, she didn't have the right to vote. Even though Van Lew wasn't the only one to hold these opinions, her letters upset many in Congress, and one by one, the few remaining supporters she had began to abandon her.

Although Van Lew's supervisor reprimanded her often, he was hesitant to fire her. Instead, he sent her a note one afternoon, shortly before she was about to leave for the day, telling her that she had been transferred to another department. Her new position—in the dead letter office—would involve heavy work and a $500 cut in pay. It was assumed, correctly, that this offer would force Van Lew to resign, and on July 11, 1887, Elizabeth, then 68 years old, returned to Richmond to make plans to live out her last years in her mansion on the hill.

Ulysses Simpson Grant

Ulysses Simpson Grant (1822–1885), like Robert E. Lee, began his military career at the U.S. Military Academy at West Point. Grant also served in the war against Mexico, from 1846–1848. Ironically, Grant did not see himself as a military man, and after the Mexican War, he left the army. But when civil war broke out, he felt it was his duty to fight, and he offered to lead a group of volunteers. He entered the war with the rank of colonel and left it as a general. He was one of the most successful military leaders of the conflict.

Three years after the war ended, Grant was nominated for president of the United States by the Republican Party. He was elected president in 1868 and again in 1872. Grant was fiercely loyal to his friends and to the men and women who had helped him during the war, and he gave many of them jobs in his administration. Unfortunately, some of Grant's appointments proved to be poor choices, and several officials were charged with graft and corruption, charges that diminished Grant's reputation.

After retiring from politics, he encountered several serious problems. A business venture failed, and Grant was forced to file for bankruptcy. Shortly afterward, he learned that he was dying from cancer. To provide some financial security for his wife, Grant frantically devoted his last days to preparing his memoirs, often writing while in great pain. *Personal Memoirs* was completed only four days before he died, and the book eventually earned more than $400,000 for his family.

Benjamin Franklin Butler

Benjamin Franklin Butler (1818–1893) was a very successful lawyer, and unlike many of the men with whom he worked during the war, he had no military background. He did have a lot of self-confidence, though, and when war broke out, he volunteered his services, believing he would be a good leader.

Although historians disagree on how successful Butler was as a general, few disagree on the fact that Southerners hated him. One of the reasons that Confederates especially detested Butler was his strict rule of New Orleans. He took command of the city after it fell in 1862, and residents thought his rule was so brutal that they called him the Butcher of New Orleans.

Also, as a Radical Republican in the House of Representatives (1866–1875) Butler wanted to take all property away from Southern soldiers who had volunteered to fight for the Confederacy, and to reward Union soldiers with land in the South. His plan did little to endear him to Southerners, even though it never passed.

He ran for several offices after leaving the House of Representatives. Sometimes he switched parties to run as a Democrat, and on other occasions, he ran as a representative of a small third party. He was elected governor of Massachusetts in 1882 after two unsuccessful attempts. He then ran, unsuccessfully, for president of the United States in 1884.

Butler returned to his legal practice in 1885, and when he died, he left an estate valued at $7,000,000.

Chapter / Eleven

The Last Years

Elizabeth moved her belongings from Washington D.C. to Richmond on July 28, 1887. She was heartsick, overwhelmed at times by feelings of betrayal and abandonment. In addition, the events of the last few years had broken her spirit. Often she seemed unsure of herself. And she was plagued by money problems.

Van Lew was still well-known—her return to Richmond was noted in the *Richmond Enquirer*—but she was not any better liked in 1887 than she had been in the 1860s. Her social activities, therefore were very limited, and she often stood by her garden gate, looking for someone to whom she might speak. She openly complained that no one loved her, and her entries in her journal were often filled with self-pity. However, the rector at

Elizabeth Van Lew seated in the garden of her Grace Street home

her church called on her often, and she attended services whenever her health permitted, so she did have some opportunities to socialize, even if they were very limited.

Even so, her social contacts did nothing to help her financial situation. Elizabeth struggled on for several years, turning down offers to buy her beloved home, hoping somehow to find a way to survive on her own. When she no longer had enough money left to buy food, she turned to friends in the North. She wrote to the sister of Paul Revere, a prisoner of war she had helped, to seek aid. Elizabeth had visited the Revere family after the war, and Revere's sister, now Mrs. John Phillips Reynolds, and Van Lew became friends. Mrs. Reynolds had made it very clear that she felt her family owed Van Lew a great deal, and if there was any way any of them might help Elizabeth, then or in the future, they would gladly do it.

As soon as Mrs. Reynolds received Van Lew's letter, she sent her son, John Reynolds Jr., to Richmond to establish a small fund for Elizabeth. This fund, to which other former prisoners or their families contributed, made it possible for Elizabeth to live in moderate comfort.

The fund also made it possible for Elizabeth to pay her property taxes and therefore to hold on to her home. Elizabeth, a fighter until the end for every cause in which she believed, sent a letter of protest along with each tax payment. She felt that she should not have to pay taxes if she couldn't vote. Why should she support a government in which she had no voice? she asked.

In the late 1800s Elizabeth's small circle of faithful servants and family members became smaller and smaller. One of her former slaves, Reed, who remained on as a servant after being given his freedom, became ill. Elizabeth cared for him in her home until he died. Then in 1895, her

Elizabeth Van Lew in 1894

brother passed away. And shortly afterward, her sister died as well.

Only a few servants, Elizabeth, and John's daughter Eliza occupied the mansion after 1895. Eliza, 40 years old, had emotional problems, and Elizabeth was very concerned about her niece's odd cleaning frenzies and was frightened by her threats of violence. Van Lew took the personal threats against her seriously, and to make it possible to get a good night's sleep, she hired a woman to stay in the mansion to make sure that Eliza remained in her room throughout the night. Yet despite Eliza's problems, Elizabeth loved her dearly, and when her niece died unexpectedly on May 10, 1900, Van Lew was devastated.

Elizabeth's health deteriorated rapidly after that, and she died early in the morning on September 26, 1900, from dropsy, a condition in which the body retains fluids. Eventually her lungs filled with water and she could not breathe. Elizabeth's sister's two daughters, one of whom lived in Philadelphia, the other in Buffalo, New York, had been notified about their aunt's failing health, and they rushed to Richmond to be with her at the end. A small service was held at St. John's Episcopal Church, and she was buried in the family's plot in Shockhoe Cemetery.

Elizabeth's Northern supporters, led by John Reynolds Jr., wanted to give Van Lew a permanent memorial. They order a huge slab of gray Massachusetts stone, which weighed more than 1 ton and measured 2 feet high and 4 feet long, to mark her grave. On this stone, they mounted a bronze plaque that read:

ELIZABETH VAN LEW
1818   1900

She risked everything that is dear to man—friends, fortune, comfort, health, life itself, all for the one absorbing desire of her heart, that slavery be abolished and the Union be preserved.

THIS BOULDER
from the Capitol Hill in Boston, is a tribute from Massachusetts friends.

Miss Lizzie would have liked it.

Chapter /Twelve

/Saving a Story

Although few people visited the Van Lew home after the war, many toured the mansion when it was opened to the public shortly after Elizabeth died. John Reynolds Jr., the executor of Elizabeth's estate, decided to put the mansion on display, hoping to find a local buyer who would value the historic home and preserve it and its contents. Many Richmonders toured the home, studying each room carefully, for there was great curiosity about the former spy and how she lived. But as the public handled her belongings, many of Van Lew's possessions were damaged and more than a few disappeared when souvenir hunters helped themselves to a memento or two. To protect the possessions that remained, the mansion was closed to the public only a month after it was opened.

To Reynold's great disappointment, there was little interest in Richmond to preserve Elizabeth's home or to start a Van Lew historical collection. So Reynolds decided to sell the mansion. It became a clubhouse for a while before being torn down to make room for a school in 1911.

Reynolds also decided to sell all of Van Lew's household furnishings. An auction, held in Boston in late November 1900, was run by John Leonard, a former prisoner of war in Richmond. More than 700 of Elizabeth's books, the desk where she wrote the messages she sent to Butler and Grant, and even the flag she flew over her house to welcome Grant's men when Richmond fell, were auctioned off for very little. The sale of all of her belongings, including her prized rosewood furniture, brought less than $1,000.

Reynolds sold many of Elizabeth's personal items as well, including her scrapbook. This book, which went to the highest bidder for $15, contained copies of passes she had used during the war, her brother's draft notice, and poetry that prisoners had written for her. It also contained autographed photos of Ulysses S. Grant and signatures of several famous people in the 1800s.

But not everything was put on the auction block. Van Lew had willed her letters, her family photos, and her wartime journal to Reynolds, and he kept these materials. He knew that many people were intrigued by Elizabeth's adventures, and he wanted to publish her journal. Apparently he had discussed this idea with Elizabeth, for she had had a copyist rewrite sections of her journal that she had originally written in great haste in nearly illegible penmanship.

When Reynolds decided not to publish her papers, he graciously allowed authors who wished to write about Van Lew to study her material. One of the first writers to do so was William Beymer, who wrote a lengthy article about Van Lew for *Harper's Monthly* in 1911. Eventually, the materials that Reynolds inherited were turned over to the Rare Manuscripts Division of the New York Public Library, where they are kept today.

At the same time that Beymer was reading Van Lew's journal, John Albree, a native of Boston, was seeking information about Elizabeth, too. After the war Albree had read newspaper articles about Elizabeth's daring escapades, and he attended the auction, where he bought several items, including John Brown's papers and several pieces of Van Lew's sterling. Owning some of Elizabeth's possessions renewed Albree's interest in Elizabeth's life, and shortly after the auction, he set out to learn more about her.

It took Albree a few years to gather the information he wanted. He traveled to Richmond to talk to people who had known her, and he hired a local photographer, H. P. Cook, to take pictures of her home, including the secret room where she hid prisoners. He also searched for names of prisoners of war in old record books and newspapers, which often listed Yankees brought into Richmond. Albree contacted many of these men, asking them to share any stories they could recall about Van Lew.

When Albree had found all he could, he prepared a lecture about Elizabeth. He was invited to present this speech at many historical societies from 1904 to 1920. Sometimes members of the audience had known Van Lew, and they gave Albree more information about her. One listener told Albree that her husband had purchased Van Lew's scrapbook, and she wondered if Albree might want to see it. Albree jumped at the chance to examine the book, then asked for—and received—permission to have a typist copy it.

Albree's materials were eventually turned over to the College of William and Mary at Williamsburg, Virginia, so that others might use the material he found. The collection includes statements about what people of the time thought about Van Lew, newspaper articles about her and her home, and a summary of family births, deaths, and marriages gleaned from official records.

If Reynolds hadn't saved Van Lew's papers and photos and if Albree hadn't talked to people who actually knew Van Lew, only a few facts found in a few newspapers would remain today. And the details of the remarkable life of a Southern belle who became a Union spy would have been lost forever.

Appendix
America's Civil War: A Time Line

Some of the major events of the Civil War period are listed below. They provide a framework for the story.

1860 December 24 South Carolina secedes. Other Southern states begin to vote on secession.

1861 April 12 The first shots of the war are fired at Fort Sumter, South Carolina.

April 15 Union president Abraham Lincoln prepares to use massive force against the Confederacy (the seceded Southern states).

July 21 The South wins the first battle of the war at Bull Run (also known as Manassas), Virginia.

1862 January 27 The Union starts its drive to take control of the upper South and the Mississippi River.

March 11 Union troops prepare to march on Richmond, Virginia, the Confederate capital.

April 6–7 The North encounters fierce fighting in the upper South and barely wins at Shiloh, Tennessee.

April 26 Union naval forces take New Orleans, Louisiana.

June 26–July 7 The Confederates, under General Robert E. Lee, stop the North's drive toward Richmond.

1863 July 3 A Confederate attack on the North is turned back at Gettysburg, Pennsylvania.

July 4 Union forces under General Ulysses S. Grant take Vicksburg, Mississippi, the last Confederate stronghold on the Mississippi River, after a six-week siege. Gettysburg and Vicksburg are turning points in the war. The Confederacy is seriously weakened.

1864 May 5–6 General Grant starts another Union drive toward Richmond.

May 7–December 22 Union general William T. Sherman marches from Tennessee to Atlanta and Savannah, Georgia. He destroys everything of any value to the Confederates along the way.

June 1–3 Grant encounters fierce fighting at Cold Harbor, Virginia, losing 12,000 men in one day.

June 18 Grant decides to lay siege to Richmond.

1865 January 16–March 21 Sherman marches back north through the Carolinas, again destroying anything that might help the Confederates.

April 2 The Confederates abandon Richmond.

April 9 Lee surrenders his troops to Grant at Appomattox, Virginia.

April 14 President Lincoln is shot.

April 26 The rest of the Confederate soldiers surrender to Sherman.

Bibliography

Albree, John. Papers. Earl Gregg Swem Library, College of William and Mary, Williamsburg, Va.

Beymer, William Gilmore. "Miss Van Lew." *Harper's Monthly* (June 1911): 86-99.

Bill, Alfred Hoyt. *The Beleaguered City: Richmond 1861-1865*. New York: Knopf, 1946.

Carter, Hodding. *The Angry Scar*. Garden City, N.Y.: Doubleday, 1959.

Catton, Bruce. *Never Call Retreat*. Garden City, N.Y.: Doubleday, 1965.

Channing, Steven A. *Confederate Ordeal*. Alexandria, Va.: Time-Life Books, 1984.

Corson, William. *The Armies of Ignorance*. New York: Dial Press, 1977.

Frassanito, William A. *Grant and Lee: The Virginia Campaigns, 1864-1865*. New York: Scribner's, 1983.

Hoehling, A. A., and Mary Hoehling. *The Day Richmond Died*. New York: A. S. Barnes, 1981.

Horan, James D. *Desperate Women*. New York: Putnam's, 1952.

Kane, Harnett. *Spies for the Blue and Gray*. Garden City, N.Y.: Hanover House, 1954.

Massey, Mary Elizabeth. *Bonnet Brigades*. New York: Knopf, 1966.

O'Toole, G. J. A. *The Encyclopedia of American Intelligence and Espionage*. New York: Facts on File, 1988.

Stampp, Kenneth M. *The Causes of the Civil War*. Englewood Cliffs, N.J.: Prentice-Hall, 1959.

Stuart, Meriwether. "Colonel Ulric Dahlgren and Richmond's Union Underground." *The Virginia Magazine of History and Biography* (April 1964): 152-204.

Van Lew, Elizabeth. Papers. New York Public Library.

"The War Day by Day: Fifty Years Ago." Column. *Boston Globe*, September 5, 1911-December 27, 1911.

For Further Reading

Civil War Spies

Bakeless, Katherine, and John Bakeless. *Confederate Spy Stories*. Philadelphia: Lippincott, 1973.

Burger, Nash Kerr. *Confederate Spy: Rose O'Neale Greenhow*. New York: Franklin Watts, 1967.

Reit, Seymour. *Behind Rebel Lines: The Incredible Story of Emma Edmonds, Civil War Spy*. San Diego: Harcourt Brace Jovanovich, 1988.

Wormser, Richard. *Pinkerton: America's First Private Eye*. New York: Walker and Company, 1990.

Civil War

Buchanan, Lamont. *A Pictorial History of the Confederacy*. New York: Bonanza Books, 1951.

Catton, Bruce. *This Hallowed Ground*. Special edition for young readers. Garden City, NY: Doubleday, 1962.

Meltzer, Milton, ed. *Voices from the Civil War*. New York: Thomas Y. Crowell, 1990.

/Index